Forever Investing

The Investment Strategy of History's Greatest Investors

Michael T. Nowacki

ISBN: 0692769412
ISBN 13: 9780692769416

Contents

Preface

Investing, in its many forms, existed long before the Europeans settled in America. Fortunately for America, the investment knowledge accumulated by the Europeans was imported to America with its earliest settlers; in fact, those settlers were brought by businesses funded with investor capital.

In 1584, the first expedition was led by Sir Walter Raleigh of England to establish a colony in Roanoke Island, which today is in Dare County, North Carolina. Early attempts in Roanoke failed with large casualties and community disorder. All the colonists vanished, resulting in Roanoke being dubbed the Lost Colony. To this day no one knows what happened to the colonists.

Jamestown then became the destination of colonization. The first settlement was in 1607 by a joint stock company named the London Company. A royal investigation in 1623 reported that of the six thousand migrants to Virginia since 1607, only two thousand survived. The average life expectancy after arriving was a mere two years.[1]

The London Company, New Plymouth Company, and Massachusetts Bay Company are largely responsible for organizing the earliest British colonies in what is now the United States. In other words, entrepreneurs and investors are not only the driving force of our economy today, but they also played a pivotal role in the early settling of the United States.

Life during the early settling of the United States through the Industrial Revolution in late nineteenth century continued to be extremely challenging for individuals and families. People were faced with indentured servitude, slavery, low wages, poor-quality health care, unclean water and lack of proper sewage, terrible working conditions, and very long work weeks. In 1900 the average life expectancy was still only forty-seven years old, largely due to high infant-mortality rates and a lack of adequate medical treatments.

Technological advances in agriculture and the Industrial Revolution moved us from an agrarian economy to manufacturing and services. The Industrial Revolution—and economic progress made thereafter—vastly improved living standards, working conditions, medical care, and nutrition. In fact, John D. Rockefeller Sr. and Andrew Carnegie were the richest men in the United States, and in 1900 even they couldn't buy penicillin, x-rays, insulin, central heat and air conditioning, cell phones, televisions, computers, or fly in commercial airplanes, because these things weren't available. In many ways the middle class today has a much higher living standard than the richest people in the world who lived a hundred years ago.

There have been some world-changing breakthroughs in the last few decades, such as the mapping of the human genome and ARPANET (the predecessor to the modern Internet), which were accomplished by academics and research institutions. However, it has been entrepreneurs and businesses that were responsible for the vast majority of the new scientific, medical, and technological advances that improved our standard of living. New drugs, medical devices, smartphones, electric cars, Amazon, Google, credit cards, Internet servers, online banking, and Microsoft Office are just a tiny sample of the businesses that have improved our standard of living in the last few decades.

Businesses are the primary driving force of our economy. If it weren't for businesses, there wouldn't be any jobs, and the government would shut down from having no revenue source. Our Founding Fathers created a brilliant political system that promoted free enterprise, property rights, and little regulation, which allowed entrepreneurs to thrive. Our government also benefits from this system by collecting the highest tax revenues of any country in the world, roughly $6.5 trillion annually.

Entrepreneurs and the government play a critical role in the economy, but so do investors. Investors are the people who fund entrepreneurs' new businesses and help existing businesses to expand. Investors also fund government spending through the purchase of government bonds. For example, consider the War Bonds issued by the US government during World War II. Over the course of the war, eighty-five million Americans purchased bonds totaling approximately $185 billion.

We were also recently reminded in 2007–2009 how important it is to have investors and liquidity in credit markets.

When investors fled the credit markets from 2007–2009, the Treasury Department and Federal Reserve had to step in to provide liquidity and keep the economy functioning—without investing the economy shuts down. Fed Chairman Ben Bernanke and Treasury Secretary Hank Paulson are the heroes who made tough, unpopular, and wise decisions during one of the most dangerous times in American economic history.

Scientists, inventors, entrepreneurs, investors, government, and a productive workforce facilitate the growth in our economy and improve our standard of living. As an investor, you should be cognizant of your economic role and feel a sense of contribution.

While investing has been around since ancient civilization, investing into publicly traded stocks has only become popular in the last century. Prior to the booming market in the 1920s, very few households and institutions invested into common stocks.

Over the past one hundred years, there have been many strategies developed for investing into *stocks*, but investing into *businesses* has not changed. Business flippers (i.e., most stock investors) own companies for a few years at most and then sell them for a quick profit. Business owners, on the other hand, intend to own the business forever. Whether it is a private or a publicly traded business, owners of businesses make purchases, because they believe the intrinsic value will be much higher in the future.

The quicker you get divorced after your wedding, the bigger the mistake you probably made in selecting a spouse. Businesses are not much different: the quicker you sell it, the bigger the mistake you probably made in your purchase. The best investments are the ones you stay with for the rest of your life. They are *forever investments*.

Notes

1. Gary M. Walton and Hugh Rockoff, *History of the American Economy*, 11th ed. (Mason, OH: South-Western, Cengage Learning, 2010), 28.

Introduction

Passionately and eloquently arguing for a position does not make it true, even if it is done with great persuasion. It is a sad reality that sophisticated foolishness often draws bigger crowds than sober wisdom. For those capable of being influenced, the presentation often carries more weight than the argument.

The merits of forever investing are supported by strong empirical evidence and advocated by many of history's most successful investors. As a first-time author, I hope that I've made a compelling case in favor of forever investing because—if successfully executed—it is the most effective strategy for investors. If you finish the book unconvinced, it is my failing as a writer and not that of the strategy.

While we are blessed to have the freedom to choose our future profession, one of life's great tragedies is that we have to decide what type of work we want to do for the rest of our life at eighteen or nineteen years old, but we have no experience in the fields we are considering. How do we know if we'll enjoy something if we've never done it?

Eighteen years ago I was trying to figure out my own career path. There were two things I wanted in a career: (1) opportunity for advancement and (2) a feeling of contribution to society. Nurses, teachers, firefighters, and police officers definitely fit the second need, but the opportunity to move up in those careers is limited.

The book *Titan: The Life of John D. Rockefeller Sr.* came out the year before and was still displayed at bookstores. I was born and raised in the Cleveland, Ohio area, and that made me particularly attracted to Rockefeller, who also grew up in Cleveland. While I was fascinated with Standard Oil's serial acquisitions of competitors to build a monopoly, it was his philanthropic accomplishments that were inspiring. What a great way to spend the late years of your life: giving away a fortune to eradicate diseases, build colleges and universities, support churches, and fund medical research.

At that point, I determined that I wanted to become a philanthropist. Of course, to give away a great fortune, you have to create one in the first place. I read everything I could get my hands on about becoming wealthy. The Forbes 400 list was a valuable starting point.

After eliminating the people who inherited their wealth, nearly everyone left on the list was an entrepreneur or investment manager. While entrepreneurship was the most common path to the Forbes 400 list, for those without great start-up ideas, investing is the surer way to wealth.

My introduction to investing coincided with the Tech bubble bursting, which made it an interesting time to learn about the stock market. Instantly I was drawn to Warren Buffett; his track record and net worth made him a credible source of investment advice, but it was also his ability to explain things using common sense language and wit.

At the age of twenty-three, I began managing investment accounts for family members and friends based on Warren Buffett's investment approach. I bought great companies that I believed would increase in intrinsic value over time: UnitedHealth Group, MBNA, Home Depot, and a handful of others. These were strong companies, in good industries, and arguably the best businesses in their industry. The stocks performed very well for my investors.

While earning my master's degree in financial economics at Ohio University, my professor who taught international finance learned of my passion for investing and called me into his office. A few years earlier, the professor, John Puthenpurackal, had coauthored an academic paper that showed if you mimicked Berkshire Hathaway's stock portfolio from 1976–2006 (it was updated to 2006 a few years after we met) when the holdings became public information, you would have earned a 51,399 percent return, or 12.7 times the return in the S&P 500 with dividends.[1]

Professor Puthenpurackal and I went over his portfolio, and I thought it was made up of good businesses. I made one recommendation: buy Chipotle. It was just spun off from McDonald's, and people were crazy about the burritos, especially people in their twenties and thirties. There was even a Facebook group called something along the lines of "Ohio University Students for Chipotle" asking Chipotle to open a location on campus (there is one on campus today). The valuation was attractive when you consider how rapidly it could grow its store count in the future, and it had close ties with the best management in the business, McDonald's, who announced they intended to still own a position in the company. I made the stock my largest position but was impulsive and sold it after a quick 50 percent gain in a few months. Then I bought it again during the financial crisis and made a 100 percent gain in a short period, but foolishly sold it another time because I thought the valuation was high. I am not sure if my old professor held on to the stock, but it has risen more than ten-fold since the recommendation ten years ago. *If you get one thing from this book, it is that if you find a once-in-a-decade opportunity like Chipotle, buy a lot of it and don't sell just because the stock went up quickly.*

After earning my master's degree, I went job hunting, but I didn't like the job opportunities that were available to me. I was a great student, worked my tail off, and earned excellent grades; however, I was introverted my whole life and at the time lacked great social skills, which are crucial to succeed in the corporate world. The few opportunities I was offered were essentially to be a mutual-fund salesman for large advisory firms. Given my weak social skills at the time, the offers are indicative of how desperate advisory firms are for salespeople. I turned down the offers and opened a new-and-used bookstore.

The margins on used books, CDs, and DVDs are gigantic. I learned this when I went to a local Half Price Books. I brought in some economics best sellers and received $0.15 to $0.25 a book. Then I saw them on the shelf for $6 a week later. Since Half Price Books was approaching one hundred stores nationwide, I thought it must be a good business. People always advise "Do what you love!" and I love reading, so I believed it was a perfect fit.

So, with no retail work experience in my life, in 2007 I started a bookstore with the intention of opening dozens more in the future. The first three years were the hardest I've ever worked, putting in thirteen-hour days, six days a week. I work long hours today, but reading 10-Ks and conference-call transcripts is much different than working on your feet in retail.

During the first few years, things at the bookstore went well, but every year Amazon became more popular, and the Kindle exploded onto the scene. Borders went bankrupt in 2011, and my business partner and I went around to a few Borders locations, buying up the inventory. This provided a short-term boost to our sales and profits, but the economics of the industry had changed. Bookstores were now a terrible business.

In 2008, the housing bubble collapsed, and the stock market followed. The portfolios I managed for family members and friends declined rapidly, but fortunately they did not panic. I used the opportunity to invest more of my personal money into the market and even took out a loan to take advantage of the rare opportunities. In 2009, I earned a 286.74 percent return on my money. It was almost all short-term gains, and it felt much less impressive when my accountant told me how much I owed in taxes.

In 2011, the bookstore was no longer doing well. Investing was my real passion, so I decided to start an investment-advisory business with a focus on value investing. I only had a tiny base to start with of $1 million in assets under management.

Things went well, and performance at my firm was great the first few years through 2014, returning 107 percent (net of fees), while the S&P 500 Total Return index returned 64 percent. Word of mouth spread, and my assets under management grew far faster than I anticipated—nearly twenty-fold in three years. Then, in late-2014 some of my large investments tumbled. I was crushing the market all throughout 2014, but with the terrible last few months I only finished within a few basis points of the S&P 500 Total Return.

In 2015, I was hoping for a strong year, but it ended up being a poor year. The S&P 500 ended the year relatively flat, meanwhile most stocks that looked undervalued turned out to be value traps, and their stock prices plummeted. It was widely publicized that billionaire Bill Ackman was down 20 percent for that year. Billionaire fund manager David Einhorn had only one negative year since he founded his firm in 1996, but he was down 20 percent in 2015 as well. Also in 2015, billionaire value investor Seth Klarman's hedge fund was reported to have had only his third negative year in thirty-three years. It was a tough year, and I had excellent company, but it did not excuse my poor performance and mistakes. I was embarrassed and frustrated.

With everything going wrong, I became determined to find the problems in my investment approach and do a better job of managing risks. Since 2008 I had been investing into any type of company I determined was undervalued, whether it was a microcap shipping company, a small homeowners' insurance company in Florida, Google, or IBM. I went back and looked at all my historical holdings. I reread every classic book on investing. I interviewed other talented investors about their investment approach. Along the way I discovered what went wrong: my target holding period.

Ted "10-bagger" Weschler is widely known today because he was handpicked by Warren Buffett to co-manage Berkshire Hathaway's common stock investments. Prior to working at Berkshire, Ted ran a hedge fund in Charlottesville, Virginia in a small office above a bookstore. And prior to the hedge fund he worked at a private equity firm.

I spoke with a former coworker of Ted's at the private equity firm to get a better understanding of Ted's investment approach. The former coworker said there is one difference between Ted and 99 percent of other investors: *Ted's target holding period is forever.*

After our conversation, I went and looked through Ted's holdings when he ran his hedge fund. He started his fund in 2000 and by 2012, when he closed the fund, it had a long portfolio over $2 billion. From 2000 through early 2011, a period when the market barely increased, Ted's investment performance is reported to have been over 1236 percent.[2]

Ted had a very concentrated portfolio of 10–12 stocks, with a top position sometimes making up 25 percent of his fund. He isn't concerned with short-term performance and therefore doesn't feel the pressure to sell a stock just because it went up a lot. Ted doesn't know what a stock will do in the next two years, but he is perfectly comfortable holding it if he believes it will be a much more valuable company in five years.

Ted bought a large position in W. R. Grace in 2000 when it was in bankruptcy. Years earlier, after Ted graduated from college, he worked at W. R. Grace. He understood the company well and studied the bankruptcy until he knew everything he could. W. R. Grace ended up being one of his two biggest winners and he owned it the entire time he had his fund. He reportedly made 10–20 times his money on it, but the first four years it made nothing. Most investors don't have that type of patience and conviction—they want immediate feedback.

DaVita was another stock he held for over a decade. It is tough to determine from SEC filings how much Ted paid for DaVita, but it went from a low of $1 in 2000 to over $40 in 2011. You only need one or two outstanding ideas like that in a decade to earn phenomenal returns.

After examining Ted's history I realized that the numerous examples and evidence for forever investing were right in front of my face. Andrew Carnegie was a forever investor. Warren Buffett is a forever investor. Philip A. Fisher said if an investor does his or her job, the time to sell is "almost never."[3] Benjamin Graham's most successful investment, one he said earned more money than all of his other investments combined, was a forever investment in GEICO. Entrepreneurs are forever investors. Every business that makes an acquisition does so with the expectation of owning that company forever. The Forbes 400 list is not made up of people who owned a company for a few years and sold it; it is made up of people who made their money in one, or a few, forever investments.

From 2009–2014, most of what I bought would quickly rise and the next year I'd sell it to buy another stock that appeared more attractive. I focused primarily on quantitative factors and didn't put much emphasis on the quality of the business and management team. My goal was to own the stock for two or three years and wait for the price to approach my calculation of intrinsic value, and then I'd move on.

Buying undervalued mediocre companies and having a short-term holding period of two or three years works well when we are coming out of deep recession and the intrinsic value of companies are rising. But by the end of 2013, most companies were back to operating at pre-crisis levels, and in late 2014 and 2015, when energy prices collapsed and the dollar strengthened, the intrinsic value of many companies declined.

If you own a mediocre company and it goes up quickly, you will most likely sell and try to find a more attractive opportunity, because you don't want to own a mediocre business that is fully valued. If you own a mediocre company and it declines in price, you likely won't add to it, because you don't want to own too much of a mediocre business. With this approach you will get a lot of short-term gains, and when there is inevitable weakness in the market, you'll likely be stuck with a portfolio of mediocre companies declining in price and intrinsic value. Why own poor or mediocre businesses when you can own great businesses?

Warren Buffett bought poor and mediocre companies in his early years when he was a small investor because they were cheap. He had the right amount of capital where he could take activist positions in these small companies. While he earned outstanding returns using this strategy with his fund, it didn't work so well after that. In the 1989 Berkshire Hathaway Shareholder's Letter he wrote:

> I could give you other personal examples of "bargain-purchase" folly but I'm sure you get the picture: It's far better to buy a wonderful company at a fair price than a fair company at a wonderful price. Charlie understood this early; I was a slow learner. But now, when buying companies or common stocks, we look for first-class businesses accompanied by first-class managements.

In a rising market, everything you buy will immediately go up and your decisions feel validated. In a flat or declining market, a stock may drop immediately after being acquired and you will need considerable patience. Intelligent investors want to own a portfolio of great companies with exceptional management when patience is required.

When you perform a valuation of a company it is based on all-future cash flows. However, if you are only investing in that company for a few years, your investment horizon is not consistent with that of your valuation methods.

An investor that only holds a stock for a few years is a short-term investor hoping the market will recognize the perceived dislocation of value during the brief time he or she is willing to own the stock. On the other hand, an investor over two decades can expect a return similar to the growth in intrinsic value of the business, plus the change in the multiple. Too many investors misapply the title of long-term investor to their investment approach. If you have 100 percent turnover, for twenty consecutive years, you are not a long-term investor; *you are a short-term investor for a long time.*

Forever investing is not for everyone. Some investors lack the skills and expertise to identify outstanding companies. Others lack the patience and temperament that is required. This book was written to make a case for forever investing and provide the framework for those who wish to pursue it.

It is important to acknowledge that there have been some extremely talented investors who focused on short-term holding periods. Stanley Druckenmiller, David Tepper, Peter Lynch, and Michael Steinhardt are a few short-term investors whose track records rival that of any great long-term investor. However, these investors are brilliant and had teams of analysts, traders, or co–portfolio managers. The operating infrastructure for these strategies is difficult for the average investor to replicate.

There are also extremely successful and talented investors who target companies with poor management, such as Carl Icahn and private equity investors. However, unless you can gain control of a company's board of directors and put into place your desired management team, investing into companies with poor management doesn't make much sense. Forever investing will likely appeal to investors who don't want to take over management—or don't have the means.

Investment jargon can have broad meanings, so let's get some of the semantics out of the way. Many investors refer to themselves as "buy-and-hold" investors, or "long-term" investors, but do not have a target holding period of forever. In fact, it is very rare to come across anyone who identifies himself or herself as a buy-and-hold investor who has held at least one company for over a decade.

Many so-called buy-and-hold investors overtly state that they only have a three-to five-year target holding period. Despite having "exit plans" in five to seven years, private equity firms also claim to be long-term investors. There is also the greatest misnomer of all time, *Long-Term Capital Management*, the arbitrage hedge fund in the 1990s who used excessive leverage and had to be bailed out by the Federal Reserve after nearly completely wiping out investors.

Can you imagine a CEO who makes acquisitions with a three- to five-year holding period or sells the acquired company after two years if someone offers a price that makes it fully valued? We'd label that CEO irresponsible and whimsical. We want CEOs to make acquisitions the company can own forever. Likewise, forever investors are owners of businesses, not traders of businesses.

Notes

1. Gerald S. Martin, American University. John Puthenpurackal, University of Nevada, Las Vegas. *Imitation is the Sincerest Form of Flattery: Warren Buffett and Berkshire Hathaway.* Research updated April 15, 2008.

2. Carol Loomis, "Meet Ted Weschler: Buffett Auction Winner, Berkshire's New Hire," *Fortune.com,* September 12, 2011.

3. Philip A. Fisher, *Common Stocks and Uncommon Profits* (New York: John Wiley & Sons, Inc., 1996), 85.

Chapter One

Suitability

While the stock market will likely produce better returns than other asset classes over time, it is not the place for everyone. People with short-term investment horizons or those who can't tolerate volatility are especially not suitable for investing into publicly traded businesses.

In the short-term the stock market can be flat, steadily rising, or have wild swings; it is unpredictable. However, over long periods of time, the stock market will do very well and you can earn market returns by simply investing into a stock market index fund. For those investors who want to earn returns above that of the market, you must be willing to accept frequent short-term underperformance in order to achieve above-average long-term outperformance.

Many people choose to hire investment professionals to make their investment decisions. There are three reasons to hire someone to handle your decision-making: (1) you don't have the expertise, (2) you don't have the talent, or (3) you don't have the right psychological makeup and need someone to calm you during market ups and downs. Money managers impolitely refer to the third reason as client "hand holding." The more polite (or egotistical) money managers call themselves "financial psychologists."

When you meet with an investment advisor, keep in mind that most of them are not talented investors. Evidence of this is in their propensity to heavily invest client money into actively managed mutual funds. What exactly is a mutual fund? It is a pooled investment vehicle run by *another* investment manager that is charging fees—usually 0.8 percent to 1.5 percent of your assets annually. In other words, you go to your advisor for his or her help in investing, then your advisor goes to a mutual-fund manager for help. And your advisor will usually charge you over 1 percent annually for this service.

The job of the advisor is primarily to find out what investment products are suitable for you and then allocate your money based on their models—the same models found on Morningstar or Schwab for free. "Modest returns with low volatility" is the investment plan most investment advisors recommend, partly because the more an advisor convinces clients to avoid volatility and accept lower returns, the easier the advisor's job becomes. What the advisor won't do, however, is lower his or her fee for you as they lower your expected return. A client who pays his or her advisor 1 percent of assets under management, but only earns 5 percent a year, will be paying 20 percent of the profits to the advisor. A client who pays 1 percent but earns 10 percent annually, will be paying 10 percent of the profits to the advisor.

I'm not suggesting that advisors recommend clients be more aggressive; I'm recommending advisors lower their fees. (Note: *Thrifty Investing*, which is a traditional advisory firm that focuses on suitability, charges no management fees on equity accounts to clients under $25,000, 1 percent for clients between $25,000 and $1 million, and 0.75 percent on anything above $1 million. For income accounts we charge a flat rate of 0.5 percent. For more information, go to www.thriftyinvesting.com.)

In investing, how you earn your returns matters just as much as what returns you earn. Taking huge risks and getting lucky is not a viable and repeatable investment approach. A gambler can play roulette and bet on black or red and earn a 100 percent return in a few seconds; however, the person was not talented just because he or she earned a high return. If the gambler lost, it would've resulted in a loss of 100 percent. It is important to distinguish between the lucky speculator and the talented investor.

Conversely, there is a plethora of money managers whose investment philosophy is to manage volatility and target consistent annual returns of 5–7 percent (i.e., absolute return funds). However, many of these money managers experience significant underperformance when the market has a good year and are still very volatile when the market has a poor year— albeit less volatile than the market. Giving up a lot of long-term returns for a little less volatility doesn't make much sense for the long-term investor.

Talented investors not only earn above-average returns, they are above average at risk management. Risk is defined as (1) the probability of losing money and (2) the amount of money you can lose. Keep in mind that if your investment horizon is long enough, the stock market is essentially risk-free. If your investment horizon is too short, the stock market is a casino.

Many major asset classes perform in-line with inflation over long periods, including real estate, gold, and government bonds. In fact, with housing making up 40 percent of the Consumer Price Index, you'd expect a strong correlation between real-estate returns (without leverage) and inflation. The stock market may be more volatile than other asset classes, but if you have a twenty-year investment horizon, why care about monthly fluctuations? If you have shorter than a ten-year investment horizon, you probably shouldn't be invested into stocks.

Investment Philosophies

There are many different ways to make money by investing into businesses. Andrew Carnegie, Benjamin Graham, Peter Lynch, Carl Icahn, George Soros, Michael Steinhardt, David Tepper, Stanley Druckenmiller, and Warren Buffett all invested very differently from each other, yet each earned outstanding returns.

There is definitely a need for different investment styles too. For example, if investors only invested into high-quality companies, no one would invest into low-quality companies. The low-quality companies would then become extremely undervalued and have trouble raising capital. In other words, we need bargain hunters who don't want to own a company forever to keep the market more efficient.

We also need people who are willing to make speculative investments into young companies. Early investors into Starbucks, Amazon, Microsoft, Google, and Facebook were taking a big risk at the time. When Amazon was in its first year, founder Jeff Bezos told investors they had a 70 percent chance of losing their money. New businesses need investors who can accept those odds.

While I make the case for forever investing, it is not the best investment strategy for everyone. The best investment strategy for you depends on your knowledge, passion, and talent. Donald Trump grew up in a family that owned a lot of real estate and it makes sense for him to have become a real-estate investor. Bill Gross and Jeffrey Gundlach are great fixed-income mutual-fund managers and it makes sense for them to put most of their investable assets into fixed income. Bruce Karsh, the Chief Investment Officer of Oaktree Capital Management, has spent his career managing vehicles that invest into distressed debt, so it makes sense if he invests much of his own assets into distressed debt.

Bargain hunting, or value investing, is very popular today. These investors typically have a short-term investment horizon of one to five years for each holding. Bargain hunters look to purchase businesses that aren't good long-term investments, but are very cheap. They hope the market recognizes the companies are undervalued and the bargain hunters can sell at a quick profit in one to five years.

Growth at a reasonable price (GARP) is also a popular investment strategy. Peter Lynch is considered to have been a GARP investor, but that is a mischaracterization because he invested into all six types of common stocks and made his most money in cyclicals. Buffett is the most recognized practitioner of GARP, even though I've never heard him mention the acronym (perhaps because GARP sounds more like a fish than an investment philosophy). There are both short-term investors and forever investors who use GARP, but it is most consistent with forever investing.

Private-equity investors take a different approach to investing in businesses than the typical investor in common stocks. Private-equity investors manage risk by gaining control over management decisions and the trade-off is that the investment is often illiquid for the first five to seven years. Private-equity investors also often use debt to leverage their investment and increase their return on investment. Due to the benefits of leverage, successful private-equity investors earn returns that most common stock investors envy.

An entrepreneur is someone who puts "all his or her eggs in one basket" and the Forbes 400 list is almost entirely composed of these individuals. You won't find any "self-made" people on the Forbes 400 list that invested his or her own money and created a fortune through Modern Portfolio Theory, day-trading, or wide diversification among asset classes. Steve Jobs, for example, is famous for his accomplishments at Apple. However, Jobs earned most of his fortune from his investment in Pixar. In 1986, after recently being forced out of Apple, Jobs invested $10 million into Pixar. He later put in another $50 million. Jobs owned roughly 51 percent of Pixar when it was sold to Disney in January of 2006 for $7.4 billion in Disney stock. Jobs didn't cash out though and diversify. He kept the Disney shares he received as payment and Disney stock went from $22 on the day the acquisition was announced to over $100 in 2015 (his trust still owns the shares).

What to Expect When Investing into Stocks

The most attractive characteristic of investing into the stock market is that the odds are in your favor. If you simply perform in-line with the market, the odds of losing money over a twenty-year period are essentially zero.

Over a thirty-year period you should expect to do better owning businesses than owning bonds, gold, unleveraged real estate, or most other asset classes. Trying to time when other asset classes will outperform businesses has not been a reliable strategy for most investors. If your investment horizon is thirty years or longer, it makes sense to put most of your assets into businesses and ignore the volatility.

In the short-term there are numerous variables that impact a stock price: market sentiment, earnings expectations, sales expectations, interest rates, the global economy, and so on. Over a twenty-year period there are two things that predominantly determine the price movement of a stock: (1) the growth of intrinsic value and (2) the change in the multiples.

US Timeline of Recessions and War

Historically there have been long stretches of time when the market made investors much wealthier, but there have also been stretches of time when the market performed poorly. If you invested into the US stock market in 1928, you would have had to endure fourteen recessions, including the Great Depression and 2007–2009 financial crisis. You would have also invested during World War II, the Korean War, the Cold War, Vietnam, and the Gulf Wars.

Stock Market Crash of 1929
Great Depression 1929–1933
Recession of 1937–1938
Pearl Harbor, and United States enters World War II
Recession of 1945
Recession of 1949
Korean War 1950–1953
Recession of 1953
Recession of 1958
Recession of 1960–1961
Bay of Pigs Invasion in Cuba 1961

Vietnam War 1965–1973
Recession of 1969–1970
1973–1975 recession
1980 recession
Early 1980s recession 1981–1982
Early 1990s recession 1990–1991
Gulf War 1990–1991
2001 recession
War in Afghanistan 2001–present
Iraq War 2003–2011
Great Recession 2007–2009

Despite the many conflicts and short-term economic challenges, if you invested $100,000 in 1928, you would have had $290 million at the end of 2014.

Period	Annualized Returns	Cumulative Returns
1928–1932	−12.7%	−49%
1933–1936	30.1%	187%
1937–1941	−8.4%	−36%
1942–1945	24.6%	141%
1946–1948	0.6%	2%
1949–1965	16.3%	1202%
1966–1974	0.1%	1%
1975–1999	17.1%	5083%

2000–2008	−3.6%	−28%
2009–2014	17.0%	157%
Total	9.60%	289940%

Source of Data: Aswath Damodaran, professor, NYU (http://pages.stern.nyu.edu/~adamodar/New_Home_Page/datafile/histretSP.html)

Over the past fifteen years, if you have invested into stocks, you likely saw your portfolio drop 50 percent from its highs *two times*. If you have a long-term investment horizon, the drops should not cause you serious concern because the market has always recovered. However, if you are invested into stocks and need that money within a few years, a 50 percent drop will cause anxiety and may result in severe financial losses.

Over thirty-year periods the stock market will move in-line with the growth in earnings of companies that make up the market. If you examine a chart of the S&P 500 relative to S&P 500 earnings growth, it shows a clear long-term correlation between the S&P 500 earnings and its price level. There are periods, such as the late 1990s and 2009, when there is a large disconnection between price and earnings, but over time the two move together.

The key takeaways to always keep in mind about the stock market are that (1) in the long-term the S&P 500 returns are likely to equal S&P 500 earnings growth plus dividends, (2) the timing of your investment into the market and your exit from the market have an impact on your investment returns, and (3) in the short-term anything can happen.

Predicting the Stock Market

One of the most common questions professionals in the investment industry hear is "What do you think the market will do this year?" The honest answer is: "I have no idea because it's impossible to predict." However, that is not what clients like to hear, and therefore professionals give their opinions about what "should" happen.

What "should" happen is based on market sentiment, the direction of interest rates, corporate earnings, and the price-levels of the market. But what "should" happen is rarely what does happen.

Economic and Industry Changes

Throughout this book I purposely refer to forever investing as having a *target* holding period of forever. In reality, some of our investments won't live up to our expectations and should be sold—it is only our greatest investments that we should own forever. Industries, operations, balance sheets, and management teams change over time and these may cause us to sell a business.

Industries have drastic changes over multi-decade periods. If you examine the largest industries in the United States and United Kingdom in 1900 and 2015, you will see the relative size of industries change substantially over time. For example, in 1900 railroads made up the majority of market share out of the top one hundred companies. At the time, investors couldn't fathom the future impact diesel trucks and airplanes would have on the industry.

A common mistake among investors is the pursuit of growth industries, rather than growth businesses. A fast-growing industry does not necessarily lead to strong earnings for the companies within that industry. In fact, fast-growing industries tend to attract a lot of entrants and competition becomes cut-throat. In recent years, 3-D printing and solar energy were "hot" industries with tremendous potential, but the products have failed to bring in adequate levels of free cash flow and attract enough demand.

In the early 1900s, it was clear that the automobile industry was going to be the industry of the future due to rapidly rising demand. While demand for automobiles met expectations, the industry has been plagued by strong competition, regulatory barriers, costly pensions and benefits for employees, and highly cyclical revenues.

In 1900, just one in every ninety-five hundred Americans owned an automobile; 40 percent were steam powered, 38 percent were electric, and 22 percent were powered by gasoline burnt in an internal combustion engine. In 1902, at least fifty firms in the United States began manufacturing automobiles. Between 1904 and 1908, over 240 more companies in the United States were established to manufacture automobiles.[1] In recent years there were only three dominant domestic automobile companies: General Motors, Chrysler, and Ford. In 2009, Chrysler and General Motors both filed for bankruptcy protection, wiping out shareholders and reorganizing under Chapter 11 Bankruptcy Code. A new rival with luxurious electric cars has also entered the industry: Tesla Motors.

Banking is also a fiercely competitive and highly regulated business, so why has banking done so much better than the auto industry? One reason is because making automobiles is very capital intensive; companies typically spend all their profits each year on plants, property, and equipment. Banks, on the other hand, require very little reinvestment of profits to maintain their competitive position and the profits they make can be used to expand operations, acquire other businesses, issue dividends, or repurchase shares.

Another reason for the difference is that automobiles are highly cyclical businesses, while banking is mildly cyclical. In good years the automobile companies pay shareholders a dividend and take on debt to pay for capital expenditures. Then, when the economy is in a recession the automobile industry suffers massive losses that wipe out many prior years of profitability, forcing the companies to cut dividends and scramble to pay the large debt obligations.

The most durable businesses and industries are those that have sustainable demand, require low-capital expenditures, earn high returns on invested capital, and generate the high levels of free cash flow. Understanding long-term industry fundamentals are important for entrepreneurs, employees, creditors, and equity investors.

Businesses Are Not Static

The Dow Jones Industrial Average (DJIA) is a composite consisting of thirty of the largest, safest stocks in the United States. However, if you look at the companies in the DJIA over time, you will see that many don't survive and very few continue to thrive.

Businesses and industries are not static; they are constantly changing, evolving, or disappearing. You cannot "buy-and-forget." You must "buy-and-observe." Companies report quarterly financials, and as a business owner, you should be reading the reports and listening in on the shareholder conference calls.

Once you hold ownership of a business, you must continuously examine the industry conditions and the operations of the business. When you see weakness, you must also be able to distinguish between short-term challenges that will be overcome and permanent deterioration. Monitoring on a quarterly or semiannual basis will help you determine when you should buy more equity in that business or if you should ultimately exit the business.

Dow Jones Industrial Average

April 21, 1899	January 29, 1930
The American Cotton Oil Company	Allied Chemical and Dye Corporation
Federal Steel Company	General Foods Corporation
The Peoples Gas Light and Coke Company	Paramount Publix Corporation
American Steel & Wire Co.	American Can Company
General Electric Company	General Motors Corporation
Tennessee Coal, Iron and Railroad Company	Radio Corporation of America

28

The American Sugar Refining Company
National Lead Company
The United States Leather Company
Continental Tobacco Company
Pacific Mail Steamship Company
United States Rubber Company

American Smelting & Refining Company
General Railway Signal Company
Sears Roebuck & Company
The American Sugar Refining Company
B.F. Goodrich Corporation
Standard Oil Co. of New Jersey
American Tobacco Company
International Harvester Company
The Texas Company
Atlantic Refining Company International
Nickel Company, Ltd.
Texas Gulf Sulphur Company
Bethlehem Steel Corporation
Johns-Manville Corporation
Union Carbide Corporation
Chrysler Corporation Mack Trucks, Inc.
United States Steel Corporation
Curtiss-Wright Corporation
Nash Motors Company
Westinghouse Electric Corporation
General Electric Company
National Cash Register Company
F. W. Woolworth Company

August 9, 1976	March 19, 2015
Allied Chemical Corporation	3M Company
Exxon Corporation	General Electric Company
Owens-Illinois, Inc.	Nike, Inc.
Aluminum Company of America	American Express Company
General Electric Company	The Goldman Sachs Group, Inc.
The Procter & Gamble Company	Pfizer Inc.
American Can Company	Apple Inc.
General Foods Corporation	The Home Depot, Inc.
Sears Roebuck & Company	The Procter & Gamble Company
American Telephone and Telegraph Company	The Boeing Company
General Motors Corporation	Intel Corporation
Standard Oil Co. of California	The Travelers Companies, Inc.
American Tobacco Company	Caterpillar Inc.
Goodyear Tire and Rubber Company	International Business Machines Corporation
Texaco Incorporated	UnitedHealth Group Incorporated
Bethlehem Steel Corporation Inco Limited	Chevron Corporation
Union Carbide Corporation	Johnson & Johnson
Chrysler Corporation	United Technologies Corporation
International Harvester Company	Cisco Systems, Inc.
United States Steel Corporation	JPMorgan Chase & Co.
E.I. du Pont de Nemours & Company	Verizon Communications Inc.
International Paper Company	The Coca-Cola Company
United Technologies	McDonald's Corporation
Eastman Kodak Company	Visa Inc.
Johns-Manville Corporation	E.I. du Pont de Nemours & Company
Westinghouse Electric Corporation	Merck & Co., Inc.
Esmark Corporation	Wal-Mart Stores, Inc.
Minnesota Mining & Manufacturing Company	Exxon Mobil Corporation
F. W. Woolworth Company	Microsoft Corporation
	The Walt Disney Company

Circle of Competence

The losses men encounter during a business life which seriously embarrass them are rarely in their own business, but in enterprises of which the investor is not the master.
—Andrew Carnegie[2]

What an investor needs is the ability to correctly evaluate selected businesses. Note that word "selected": You don't have to be an expert on every company, or even many. You only have to be able to evaluate companies within your circle of competence. The size of that circle is not very important; knowing its boundaries, however, is vital.
—Warren Buffett, 1996 Berkshire Hathaway Shareholders' Letter

Circle of competence is a phrase popularized by Warren Buffett and is a concept designed to help the investor acknowledge the parameters of his or her expertise. Overconfidence in your ability to invest into anything and everything is not a substitute for expertise. No one fully understands every business, and investing into businesses you do not understand is likely to be hazardous to your wealth.

The purpose of sticking to companies within your circle of competence is to minimize mistakes. In this respect, individual investors would be much better off following in the footsteps of corporate America. The vast majority of corporations make "tuck-in" or "bolt-on" acquisitions. These are companies purchased for the purpose of merging it into a division of the acquirer and are right in the middle of a company's circle of competence.

Of course, there are endless examples of corporate acquisitions that went wrong even when they were within the circle of competence of management. But how many more would be disappointments if companies invested outside of their circle of competence? Peter Lynch aptly described the practice of companies diversifying by acquiring businesses outside their circle of competence as "diworseification."

Ultimately, whether or not the acquisition is smart depends on the quality of the business and the price. Understanding a company and being comfortable with owning it forever does not mean it is necessarily a great investment and you can pay any price for it. Price always matters, but the circle of competence is the starting point when looking at buying opportunities. It is a critical concept to identify the universe of businesses you understand enough to purchase if the price and long-term prospects are attractive. Your circle of competence is where you must devote your attention, research, and effort.

Circle of Competence: Shelby Cullom Davis

Shelby Cullom Davis is probably the greatest investor you've never heard of. Prior to becoming a full-time investor, Shelby Davis was deputy superintendent in the New York State Insurance Department. He came to realize that insurance companies were not only great businesses that had strong long-term potential but they were also at cheap prices. In 1947, at thirty-eight years old, he quit his job and used $50,000 provided by his wife to start investing; he had no MBA or formal economics education.[3] Over the rest of his life he built a fortune estimated at $900 million.

What was unique about Shelby Davis is that he invested almost exclusively into insurance companies. He was always a passive investor and never took control of those companies. Insurance companies were his expertise and the industry had strong long-term prospects, so he focused his entire energy on that area. When US insurance stocks became expensive, he allocated capital to insurance companies in other countries, such as Japan. If Davis had diversified into industries he didn't understand as well, it is fairly certain he wouldn't have done as well.

Measuring Performance

Investors have a misguided fascination with outperforming indexes every time the Earth goes around the Sun. We shouldn't let the IRS and the tax-year influence how we measure our relative performance. Mutual-fund manager Bill Miller famously beat the stock market fifteen years in a row, but he humbly admits that this remarkable streak was only because of the calendar year. If you look at his twelve-month performance by using different months to start the twelve-month period, there were some twelve-month periods of underperformance.

When investing your own money you will likely be OK with three straight years of underperformance if you are completely confident that your strategy, holdings, and talent will produce significant long-term outperformance. However, if you are a mutual-fund manager you might be dropped to one-star or two-stars from Morningstar and lose assets under management. If you are a hedge fund, clients might redeem their money citing high fees for underperformance. In other words, there is tremendous pressure on money managers for short-term performance, which can be disadvantageous in terms of risk-taking and taxes.

As an investor you should strive for strong long-term "absolute returns" and "relative returns." Absolute returns are important because that is what makes your net worth go up. However, relative returns are also important because if you can't beat an index, such as the S&P 500, over long periods of time, you should invest into an index fund. In that respect, the index fund is your opportunity cost.

For long-term investors it's better to underperform the market one out of three years and earn 12 percent annual returns, than to have down years one out of ten years and earn 8 percent returns. Volatility and short-term underperformance is not the same thing as risk.

For business owners, the measure of results should be based on two criteria. One is the increase in intrinsic value of the company, as measured by earnings, free cash flow, or tangible book value. The second is the increase in the company's competitive position in its market.

Notes

1. *The Automobile Industry 1900–1909*, The History of American Technology, Fall 1998, http://web.bryant.edu/~ehu/h364/materials/cars/cars%20_10.htm.

2. Andrew Carnegie, *The Autobiography of Andrew Carnegie and the Gospel of Wealth* (New York: New American Library, a division of Penguin Group, 2006), 155.

3. John Rothchild, *The Davis Dynasty: Fifty Years of Successful Investing on Wall Street* (New York: John Wiley & Sons, Inc., 2001), 3.

Chapter Two

Forever Investors

Forever investors think of their investment portfolio as a holding company or conglomerate, with stocks being pieces of businesses they own. They are the purest definition of investors, with day traders being the most impure. Forever investors strictly adhere to the famous line from Benjamin Graham: "Investing is most intelligent when it is most businesslike."

Forever investing predates stock markets and throughout history there have been countless great forever investors all across the globe. A reason to study great forever investors is to learn what has worked and not worked, then use this knowledge to create a better investment process. There are three investment strategies that forever investors favor: the Four Filters, platform companies, and start-ups.

The Four Filters

Two of the most well-known investors are Warren Buffett and Charlie Munger, who began their careers investing into poor businesses that were undervalued, which they didn't want to own for long. As they became wiser and more experienced, they changed their investment approach to high-quality companies that they could own forever. Buffett and Munger even created a framework to aid them in identifying great forever investments: The Four Filters.

These Four Filters are designed to mitigate risks through minimizing uncertainty. The goal is to identify companies that will increase in intrinsic value at a strong pace over time and are selling at attractive prices. The Four Filters have been repeatedly emphasized by Warren Buffett and Charlie Munger since the 1977 Berkshire Hathaway shareholder's letter nearly forty years ago:

> We select our marketable equity securities in much the same way we would evaluate a business for acquisition in its entirety. We want the business to be (1) one that we can understand, (2) with favorable long-term prospects, (3) operated by honest and competent people, and (4) available at a very attractive price. We ordinarily

make no attempt to buy equities for anticipated favorable stock-price behavior in the short term. In fact, if their business experience continues to satisfy us, we welcome lower market prices of stocks we own as an opportunity to acquire even more of a good thing at a better price.

Our experience has been that pro-rata portions of truly outstanding businesses sometimes sell in the securities markets at very large discounts from the prices they would command in negotiated transactions involving entire companies. Consequently, bargains in business ownership, which simply are not available directly through corporate acquisition, can be obtained indirectly through stock ownership. When prices are appropriate, we are willing to take very large positions in selected companies, not with any intention of taking control and not foreseeing sell-out or merger, but with the expectation that excellent business results by corporations will translate over the long term into correspondingly excellent market value and dividend results for owners...

Berkshire Hathaway's stock returns over the first fifty-year period after Buffett took over were 21.6 percent compounded annually. In other words, when executed successfully, forever investing based on the Four Filters can result in very high returns over long periods of time. It can also be done with very small long-term risk. In the 2014 Berkshire Hathaway Shareholder Letter, Buffett wrote about how low-risk it can be if well executed:

In the past 50 years, we have only once realized an investment loss that at the time of sale cost us 2% of our net worth. Twice, we experienced 1% losses. All three of these losses occurred in the 1974-1975 period, when we sold stocks that were very cheap in order to buy others we believed to be even cheaper.

Platform Companies

A platform company is a business an investor acquires with the intention of using the cash flow to make future acquisitions in that same industry. Future acquisitions aren't necessarily direct competitors of the platform company; they are often complementary businesses or suppliers. Whenever you hear of a company making a "bolt-on acquisition" or "tuck-in acquisition" in the same industry, it is creating a greater platform.

When Facebook had its IPO in 2012 many investors scoffed at the valuation. While I didn't purchase the stock, I pointed out to others that the IPO price may be justified or even undervalue the company. My argument was that Facebook would likely use its high stock to acquire other young companies with complementary businesses. Since its founding in 2005, Facebook has made over fifty acquisitions, including WhatsApp and Instagram. Despite the many investors who argued Facebook was overvalued at the IPO in May 2012, the shares have more than tripled in its first four years as a publicly traded company.

There is a difference between a conglomerate—such as Berkshire Hathaway, General Electric, Icahn Enterprises, Leucadia—and platform companies. A conglomerate will acquire unrelated businesses in entirely different industries, while platform companies make purchases within their industry. Standard Oil building its oil refining monopoly through consolidation is the prime example of a platform company.

Start-ups

Entrepreneurs are forever investors and many of their investors are as well. There are different names given to these early investors—venture capitalists, seed investors, angel investors—but we can generalize and call them investors in start-ups. Andrew Carnegie and the Mellon brothers have two of the best track records in United States as early-stage investors.

Forever Investor Profiles

> Much of what you become in life depends on whom you choose to admire and copy.
> —Warren Buffett, 2015 Berkshire Hathaway
> Shareholders Letter

Warren Buffett is one of the most recognized and vocal of the forever investors. He is widely quoted throughout this book and his story is well-known by all investors; therefore, rather than being redundant, I will introduce readers to forever investors who aren't as well-known. Ted Weschler, the wildly successful fund manager who now works at Berkshire Hathaway, has also been covered in the Introduction and will not be covered again.

One investor with ties to Berkshire Hathaway who does deserve mentioning is David Gottesman. If you invested into Berkshire in 1965, by the end of 2015 you would have earned a 1,598,284 percent return. That sounds like a no-brainer in hindsight, but according to Buffett, Berkshire's share price declined 50 percent three separate times in those fifty years. In other words, no matter how great the company, there will be many times you are tempted to sell based on market conditions, short-term fundamentals, and other factors.

Being a forever investor requires unwavering conviction in the quality of the company and management. It also requires the right psychological makeup to stick with a company when it is underperforming in the short-term.

David Gottesman is the forever investor we all dream about becoming. He met Buffett in 1962 and became an early investor in Berkshire. David remains a large shareholder with a stake in

Berkshire worth nearly $2 billion. Imagine how foolish it would've been if he sold Berkshire at any time just because the stock was priced too high or it was underperforming. *When you find the goose that lays golden eggs, don't sell the goose.*

To avoid sounding as if forever investing is infallible and foolproof, I want to emphasize that the people profiled below are some of the top investors in the history of the United States. Everyone cannot achieve the level of success that these investors achieved, but everyone can learn from them. Your success as an investor will be determined by your execution of the strategy, not the strategy itself. When it comes to any investment approach, there is a Hall of Fame as well as a Hall of Shame. This is just a brief introduction into a tiny sample of the forever investing Hall of Fame.

Forever Investor: John D. Rockefeller Sr. (Strategy: Platform Companies)

> Don't waste your effort on a thing which ends in a petty triumph unless you are satisfied with a life of petty success. Be sure that before you go into an enterprise you see your way clear to stay through to a successful end. Look ahead. It is surprising how many bright business men go into important undertakings with little or no study of the controlling conditions they risk their all upon.
> —John D. Rockefeller[1]

Born in a small town near Ithaca, New York in 1839, John D. Rockefeller and his family moved to Cleveland in 1853 to pursue new opportunities. At sixteen years old, Rockefeller ended his schooling and began to work as a clerk at a shipping and real-estate company. At nineteen, Rockefeller grew tiresome of toiling for a menial wage. He had saved $800, borrowed another $1000, and invested in a wholesaler of produce and related goods.

40

In 1859, the discovery of oil in Titusville, Pennsylvania led to an explosion of drilling and refining. Rockefeller and a few partners leaped at the opportunity and invested capital into building a refinery in Cleveland in 1863. In hindsight, investing into oil may seem like a no-brainer, but in 1863 the automobile wasn't invented, and there were limited uses for the oil besides lighting fluid. It was a chaotic and disorganized industry in its infancy. Supply often exceeded demand, and the price fluctuations of oil were severe. In 1865, Rockefeller and his partners were having frequent disagreements and decided to put the business up for auction. The twenty-six year old Rockefeller entered the highest bid and bought out his partners.

Rockefeller was relentless in his push for efficiency, not only to increase profits, but to be protected from the wild swings of oil prices, uncertainty about supply and demand, and fierce competition. In *Random Reminiscences of Men and Events* Rockefeller spoke of the challenges:

> It is always, I presume, a question in every business just how fast it is wise to go, and we went pretty rapidly in those days, building and expanding in all directions. We were being confronted with fresh emergencies constantly. A new oil field would be discovered, tanks for storage had to be built almost overnight, and this was going on when old fields were being exhausted, so we were therefore often under the double strain of losing the facilities in one place where we were fully equipped, and having to build up a plant for storing and transporting in a new field where we were totally unprepared. These are some of the things which make the whole oil trade a perilous one, but we had with us a group of courageous men who recognized the great principle that a business cannot be a great success that does not fully and efficiently accept and take advantage of its opportunities.[2]

At thirty-one years old, Rockefeller established the Standard Oil Co. with a few partners. It couldn't have been worse timing because 1870 and 1871 were two of the worst years in the history of the oil business. In 1871, Rockefeller said he believed that "more than three-quarters of the oil refiners in the country did a losing business." Cleveland was hit especially hard and was losing business to Pittsburgh and New York. Rockefeller, for the only recorded time in his life, became so fearful that he sold 17 percent of his shares. His brother William, who also was a partner, wrote him, "Your anxiety to sell makes me feel uneasy."[3]

It was that year, 1871, that Rockefeller came up with a strategy to combat the extreme volatility and unpredictability of the business: consolidate the industry and achieve efficiency through scale. By using this strategy, Standard Oil became one of the earliest and most successful "platform companies." Critics of Rockefeller later said he forced people to sell to him, but Rockefeller ardently refuted this and pointed out that many of the owners of the companies he bought remained with the company and became life-long partners after the mergers. The competitors who sold to Standard Oil and accepted stock as payment became wealthy if they held on, while the competitors who accepted cash later regretted not taking payment in stock. The companies that didn't sell to Standard Oil and struggled to survive in the speculative business became publicly bitter toward Rockefeller and Standard Oil.

People often carelessly attribute Rockefeller's success to being in the oil business at the right time, while not addressing the fact that he had hundreds of competitors. Moreover, some argue that Cleveland was at a geographical competitive disadvantage from other companies located in Pittsburgh and New York. What separated Rockefeller from everyone else was his ability to make strategic acquisitions and develop scale.

Rockefeller was not a wildly successful investor outside of his Standard Oil investment. He later invested into railroads, mining, real estate, steel, steamships, industrial companies, orange groves, and investment companies. The investments were handled by a small private staff and, aside from the railroads, did not produce attractive results. If John D. Rockefeller Sr. couldn't invest well when journeying beyond his circle of competence, you probably shouldn't try it either.

Rather than widely diversifying to protect his net worth once he was wealthy and retired, he kept his shares of Standard Oil— one of history's greatest forever investments. At his peak, Rockefeller is estimated to have been worth $900 million to $1 billion, arguably making him the richest person ever in relative terms.

As mentioned in the preface, John D. Rockefeller's philanthropic efforts are what inspired me to want to become an investor. Throughout history the wealthy would often leave the bulk of their fortune to heirs (e.g., Vanderbilt's and Astor's). Critics of Carnegie and Rockefeller maliciously accuse the wealthy industrialists of giving away their money to earn a more favorable public image; however, there is no evidence of this claim and wealthy businessmen before them were just as controversial and didn't give away the bulk of their fortunes. Further evidence to refute this attack on the great philanthropists is that John D. Rockefeller tithed since he earned his first paycheck at sixteen years old, many years before he became wealthy and a public figure.

In a 1932 interview, the deeply religious Rockefeller shared his views about wealth:

> I believe the power to make money is a gift from God…to be developed and used to the best of our ability for the good of mankind. Having been endowed with the gift I possess, I believe it is my duty to make more money and still more money and use the money I make for the good of my fellow man according to the dictates of my conscience.

Forever Investor: Andrew Carnegie (Strategy: Start-ups)

My advice to young men would be not only to concentrate their whole time and attention on the one business in life which they engage, but to put every dollar of their capital into it.
—Andrew Carnegie[4]

Andrew Carnegie is widely known for his steel company and establishing over twenty-five hundred libraries, but what is less known is that he was one of the greatest investors in US history.

Carnegie was born in Dunfermline, Scotland in August of 1835. He started school at the age of eight and dropped out after only four years. At twelve years old his family moved to the United States and he settled in Pittsburgh. Shortly after arriving in Pittsburgh, he began to work as a bobbin boy at a textile mill, changing spools of thread for $1.20 per week.

A year later, he began to work as a messenger boy in a telegraph office, earning $2.50 per week. Shortly thereafter, he was promoted to the position of telegraph operator and began making $20 per month.

When he was eighteen, Carnegie got his big break and took a job at Pennsylvania Railroad to become the personal telegrapher and assistant to Thomas Scott, the superintendent of the Pennsylvania Railroad's western division. Thomas Scott became Carnegie's mentor and he learned the ins and outs of the railroad industry.

Carnegie was twenty years old when his father passed away and had to step up as the primary earner in the family. The following year, Carnegie was presented with an opportunity that changed his life. Thomas Scott persuaded Carnegie to buy ten shares of Adams Express Company for $500. Carnegie didn't have the money, but his mother took out a mortgage on their home for $500 and loaned it to him. Scott then said there was a $100 premium to buy the shares and offered to loan him the money. In his autobiography, Carnegie recalled receiving his first monthly dividend check for $10: "I shall remember that check for as long as I live...It gave me the first penny of revenue from capital—something that I had not worked for with the sweat of my brow. 'Eureka!' I cried. Here's the goose that lays the golden eggs."[5]

Shortly after his Adam's Express investment, Carnegie took out a loan from a local bank and invested $217.50 in the Woodruff Sleeping Car Company. After two years, he began receiving a return of about $5000 annually, more than three times his salary from the railroad. While it may appear reckless or risky for Carnegie to buy into businesses with loans, these were joint ventures (perhaps conflicts of interest) with executives of railroads and the businesses relied heavily on railroads for growth and expansion.

In addition to his investments taking off, Carnegie was receiving promotions at work. At the age of twenty-four Carnegie became the superintendent of the Pennsylvania Railroad's western division. He was in charge of his own department and earned a salary of $1500 per year.

The following year, using money from his investment in the Woodruff Sleeping Car Company, Carnegie invested $11,000 in an oil company in Titusville, Pennsylvania. He received a return of $17,800 after only one year and over $1 million altogether from the investment.[6] Carnegie was now a wealthy man.

In 1863, at the age of twenty-eight, Carnegie's income was $42,000. About half of Carnegie's earnings came from his investment in oil, and only $2400 from his salary at the railroad. Additional investments in the Piper and Schiffler Company, the Adams Express Company, and the Central Transportation Company contributed over $13,000.

Carnegie retired from the railroad at only thirty years old. He would never again work a salaried position at a company he did not own. Carnegie and several associates then reorganized the Piper and Schiffler Company into the Keystone Bridge Company. Carnegie was keenly aware that the railroad business was booming and there was high demand to construct large bridges. He proposed building bridges with iron, rather than wood, to make the bridges more durable. Carnegie needed to invest $80,000 into the business and Thomas Scott, his former boss and mentor at the Pennsylvania Railroad, loaned Carnegie half of the money. Using his connections in the railroad business, Carnegie built the Keystone into the premier bridge maker in the country.

Despite being "retired," Carnegie remained busy. At thirty-two years old, he established the Keystone Telegraph Company with associates from the railroad industry. The company received permission from the Pennsylvania Railroad to place wire across the railroad's poles, which stretched across Pennsylvania. Within a few years, Keystone merged with the

Pacific and Atlantic Telegraph Company and Keystone's investors tripled their return.

In 1872, at the age of thirty-six, Carnegie visited Henry Bessemer's steel plants in England. The Freedom Iron Company, which Carnegie formed in 1861, had been using Bessemer's process of making steel. While in England, Carnegie realized the potential of steel and returned to America determined to expand his steel business. In 1875, Carnegie opened his first steel plant, the Edgar Thomson Works. The plant was named after the president of the Pennsylvania Railroad and, not surprisingly given the flattering gesture, the first order was for steel rails for the Pennsylvania Railroad.

In 1899, Carnegie merged several of his steel companies into Carnegie Steel. Two years later, in 1901, J. P. Morgan bought out the sixty-five-year-old Carnegie for $480 million. The purchase allowed Morgan to create US Steel and made Carnegie the richest man in the world.

Forever Investors: Andrew Mellon and Richard Mellon (Strategy: Start-ups)

Andrew and Richard Mellon were sons of Thomas Mellon, a judge in Pittsburgh who saved his money and shrewdly invested into real estate. Thomas Mellon later opened up a banking house, T. Mellon & Sons, from which he eventually stepped down and gave control over to Andrew when he was only twenty-six years old.

Thomas Mellon made early loans to Henry Clay Frick to help finance his coke business, which resulted in a relationship between the bank and Frick that lasted decades. Frick also became one of Andrew Mellon's closest friends. They were so close that in 1887 Frick left for a trip to Europe and gave his stock certificates to Andrew Mellon, telling him he had full authority to sell them as he saw fit. The two later made investments together in banking, coal, natural gas, distillery, and railroad companies.

The financial panic of 1873 caused the most prominent investment banker in the United States, Jay Cooke, to declare bankruptcy after his firm collapsed from using excessive leverage to build the Northern Pacific Railroad. It caused a severe industrial recession and massive layoffs in Pittsburgh. Nearly one half of the banks in Pittsburgh went under and T. Mellon & Sons, despite being a conservative bank, barely survived. To the eighteen-year-old Andrew Mellon, these events had a lasting impact.

The Mellon brothers owned the banking company in Pittsburgh during the late 1800s and early 1900s. While their father focused largely on real estate lending and investments, the brothers had a talent for foreseeing small companies that would eventually grow into large corporations.

In 1889, the owners of an aluminum company, the Pittsburgh Reduction Company (the predecessor to Alcoa), approached the Mellon's for a loan. The Mellon's agreed to a loan and also bought equity in the company, obtaining eleven hundred of the ten thousand shares in the company, and earning seats on the board of directors. By 1894 they raised the stake to 12.35 percent, and in 1933 the Mellon's owned 33 percent of the company.

The next major investment was in oil. Despite pushback from Standard Oil because it didn't want anyone impeding on its monopoly, the Mellon's invested $2.5 million into a 271 mile pipeline and refineries. Within a few years they were producing 10 percent of America's oil exports.[7] A few years later they sold to a Standard Oil subsidiary, for somewhere between $2.5 million to $4.5 million.[8]

Andrew Mellon then invested into the Carborundum Company, which manufactured silicon carbide, a revolutionary abrasive. It was so strong and hard it could slice through glass and tear through rock. The founder was a talented scientist, but not a good business operator. After a few years of losing money, the Mellon's replaced the founder and installed a new CEO, who quickly turned around the company.

In 1899, the Mellon brothers, Frick, and another partner formed the Union Steel Company, which produced steel wires. The Mellon brothers invested $1 million, and three years later sold their share for between $42 million and $75 million.[9]

With the economy changing from the Industrial Revolution, the Mellon brothers found more promising opportunities. They became early investors in the New York Shipbuilding Company and the Crucible Steel Company. They bought and consolidated Pittsburgh streetcar lines. The brothers bought a mining company (Cherokee Company) and installed new management, but it didn't make much money for them. The Mellon brothers also invested with Heinrich Koppers, inventor of coke ovens which transformed industrial waste into usable products. Another early investment, and one of the most successful, was the McClintic-Marshall Construction Company, which became the greatest steel-fabricating business in the world.

The Mellon brothers were not just silent partners in their investments, they sat on the boards and kept a close eye on things. Charles Marshall, cofounder of McClintic-Marshall, called Andrew Mellon "the greatest businessman he had ever known."

The Mellon brothers also created platform companies in coal. They founded Monongahela River Coal for the boat industry and Pittsburgh Coal for railroads. Pittsburgh Coal went on a buying spree, accumulating eighty thousand acres of coal lands and five thousand railcars. Monongahela River acquired the lands, mines, coal, and steamboats of eighty-one coal and manufacturing properties. It also bought or merged with forty-four riverboat companies which owned coal ports, three thousand coal barges, and eighty steamboats. The company controlled over 70 percent of all river coal traffic. Within a few years of their founding, the two companies controlled 11 percent of US coal production.[10] However, in the long-term these two companies struggled to produce attractive returns due to high capital expenditures.

In 1901, the Mellon brothers invested into the oil business again, this time with Gulf Oil. The CEO pledged his shares in the company as collateral for a $1 million loan, but the first few years the company required heavy capital expenditures and the CEO was not able to make payments. The Mellon brothers foreclosed on the loan, took his shares, and removed him as CEO. Gulf Oil would go on to become extremely profitable.

In addition to investing into young companies with promise, the Mellon brothers were expanding within the banking industry. They eventually owned the largest banking and financial institution in Pittsburgh. Banking gave the Mellon brothers access to invest into companies, but it was the extraordinary success of their investments that made them extremely wealthy.

The Mellon brothers were two of the wealthiest people in the United States and the third-highest income-tax payers in the mid-1920s, behind John D. Rockefeller and Henry Ford. Their wealth peaked at around $300–$400 million in 1929–1930. As we saw in chapter one, someone who invested into a stock-market index in 1928 would have earned twenty-nine hundred times his or her money by the end of 2014. To put the level of their wealth in perspective, if the Mellon brothers put their $300 million net worth into an index fund that tracked the stock market, their fortunes would each be worth $870 billion today. *Forbes* estimates the family wealth today at about $11.5 billion.

Forever Investor: Benjamin Graham (Strategy: The Four Filters)

Benjamin Graham was Warren Buffett's mentor and one of the greatest investment-thinkers of all time. Graham promoted the strategy of diversifying into a group of companies that were selling below the value of its "net assets." However, Ben Graham made more money in one stock, GEICO, than in all his other investments *combined*.

In the postscript of 1971/1972 edition of *The Intelligent Investor*, Graham said GEICO did not have Wall Street appeal and his fund was offered a 50 percent interest in the company. Despite Graham being an advocate of diversification, he put 20 percent of his fund's capital into it.[11]

GEICO was an incredibly successful investment and because Graham viewed it as a "family business" he continued to own the company even when it appeared overvalued. Benjamin Graham may have been a good "value investor" or "bargain hunter," but he was most successful as a forever investor.

The lesson from Benjamin Graham is that you shouldn't be inflexible. If an once-in-a-lifetime opportunity comes along, invest heavily and hold on to it forever.

Forever Investors: Charles Koch and David Koch (Strategy: The Four Filters)

Charles and David Koch are widely known for their generous philanthropy and political activism; however, inside business circles they are known for being shrewd businessmen and talented forever investors.

Koch Industries was founded in 1940 by Fred C. Koch. His son Charles joined the business in 1961 and became president and chairman in 1966, at the age of only thirty-two. When Charles took over, his father told him that he hopes his first deal is a loser, otherwise Charles will think he is a lot smarter that he is.[12]

When Fred Koch passed away, the company was primarily owned by his four sons, with a few outside investors. Charles, David, and Bill each got just over 20 percent, while Frederick received 14 percent. After disagreeing over how the company is run, Charles and David bought their brothers' shares. Today Charles and David each own 42 percent of the conglomerate headquartered in Wichita, Kansas.

The company was renamed Koch Industries in 1968 in honor of Fred Koch. At that time it was primarily an engineering firm, owned a crude-oil-gathering-and-refining business, had minor oil-exploration interests, and owned a few cattle ranches. In the late 1960s, it had annual revenue of $250 million and 650 employees. Today Koch Industries has over $115 billion in revenue and more than a hundred thousand employees.[13]

In 1969, two years after his father passed away, Charles made an important deal that helped the company fund future acquisitions. In 1959, Fred Koch bought a 35 percent interest in Great Northern Oil Company for $5 million. It had a lucrative forty-thousand-barrels-per-day refinery. J. Howard Marshall II (who would later marry *Playboy* model Anna Nicole Smith at eight-nine years old) was the cofounder with a 16 percent stake. The other owner was an oil company in California. Charles Koch bought the 49 percent stake from the oil company in California for $30.5 million and consolidated it into Koch Industries as a wholly owned subsidiary, and then gave Marshall shares in Koch Industries. The oil refinery was later described as a cash cow that provided capital for acquisitions.[14]

Charles Koch then got the company involved in complementary businesses such as chemicals, natural gas, butane, and propane. However, he also made acquisitions into unrelated businesses such as highway and tennis court surfaces, animal feed and agriculture, and telecommunications.[15]

In April 2004, Koch Industries purchased Georgia-Pacific for $13.2 billion. While the maker of Quilted Northern toilet paper, Brawny paper towels, and Dixie Cup may seem like an odd fit for Koch Industries, it shows the Koch brothers' focus on purchasing durable businesses that they want to own forever.

As mentioned earlier, over the years Charles and David had a falling out with their brothers Bill and Frederick. After negotiations, in 1983 Koch Industries bought out Bill for $470 million and Frederick for $330 million.[16] The buyout was certainly the greatest investment Charles and David ever made.

A $10,000 investment in Koch Industries in 1960 would be worth $50 million today, which comes out to an astounding 16.75 percent compounded annual returns over fifty-five years. Koch Industries is now one of the largest privately owned companies in the world. Charles and David Koch each have an estimated net worth of $40 billion.

Forever Investor: Martin E. Franklin (Strategy: Platform Companies)

While writing this book I had the opportunity to speak with one of the most successful active investors, Martin E. Franklin. After a brief introduction into Franklin, below are some questions I had for him and the thoughtful answers I received.

Franklin is exactly the type of person you want as a CEO or Chairman: smart, ethical, big shareholder, experienced, and a great capital allocator. And despite his tremendous success as a CEO and investor, his modesty and sincerity make him disarming and approachable.

Franklin is the former CEO of Jarden; the founder and chairman of Platform Specialty Products, and the cofounder of Nomad Foods. He also sits on the board of Restaurant Brands, the parent company of Burger King and Tim Horton's, in which he owns a sizable position.

Martin E. Franklin was born in London, England and moved to a small town just north of New York City when he was fifteen years old. His father was a successful merchant banker who participated in several hostile takeovers that resulted in the breakup of conglomerates. After graduating from the University of Pennsylvania, Franklin worked for his father for four years, buying and breaking up companies. At the mere age of twenty-four he was the CEO of a company with thirteen thousand employees and responsible for selling it off in parts. This was an invaluable, hands-on experience with great responsibility. However, Franklin found it antiestablishment to break up companies and therefore inverted his father's investment strategy by acquiring and merging companies.

In 1992, Franklin bought a small chain of eye care stores for $2.3 million with partner Ian Ashken. He then merged it with a publicly traded shell company and used it to acquire or merge with other companies in the highly fragmented industry. He sold the company in 1996 for $300 million, not including spin-offs, for a twenty-three-fold return. One spin-off, Lumen Technologies, was sold two years later for $250 million.

Franklin and Ashken then set their sights on a new company. Alltrista Corporation was spun-off from Ball Corp in 1993 at $1.80 (adjusted for splits). It was a slow-growth company with old brands, and in 2001 the stock was still trading below $2. Franklin and Ashken attempted to acquire the company in 2000. They were unable to acquire the company, but accumulated 10 percent of the shares and earned board seats. Within a few months they persuaded the board to replace management. In 2001, Franklin became CEO and Ashken became CFO. The company changed its name to Jarden and laid out a strategic plan of acquiring other valuable consumer products. In the 2002 annual report, Franklin says:

> Our strategy is clear and consistent; to build a world class consumer products company that enjoys leading market shares of niche markets for branded consumable products used in and around the home. We believe this strategy has not only created a strong, vibrant platform from which to grow, but also presents a compelling investment opportunity. The nature of niche markets means they are relatively small with attractive operating margins and strong cash flows. These markets have often been neglected, providing the opportunity for positive market trends from newly invigorated management with fresh and creative ideas. We believe that many of our niche branded consumable markets share similar distribution channels which can be leveraged to include new product introductions as well as more efficient customer service.

Martin E. Franklin followed through with his strategy, making a series of acquisitions throughout the next fourteen years. Jarden was recently merged with Newell Rubbermaid at $59 a share. Since Franklin took over, investors earned over forty-five times their investment in fifteen years. Franklin's shares in Jarden converted in shares in Newell Brands, which today are worth approximately $240 million.

With backing from hedge-fund billionaire Bill Ackman, among others, Franklin founded another company in 2013 called Platform Specialty Products. The company's operations are in specialty chemicals for agriculture, industrial, electronics, packaging, automotive, and energy industries. In May 2013, Platform raised approximately $900 million in a public offering at $10 per share. In October 2013, Platform announced the acquisition of MacDermid Inc., a specialty chemical company, for $1.8 billion. Platform has subsequently acquired three businesses in the agricultural chemicals industry for approximately $5 billion.

The stock quickly rose to over $27 in 2014 after the MacDermid acquisition. However, since then a change in currency exchange rates, challenges with cultural differences at the acquired companies, and weaker demand have caused the stock to fall to a low of $6 in 2016. These are not permanent obstacles, however, they are temporary challenges.

Platform is exposed to more cyclicality than Jarden, but in the long-term that can be a positive if it makes opportunistic acquisitions during times of market weakness. Martin E. Franklin is exactly the type of manager you want to be invested with in a fragmented industry.

Franklin also cofounded Nomad Foods in 2014. In April of 2014, Nomad raised $500 million in a public offering. In April of 2015, Nomad announced the acquisition of Iglo Foods, the largest frozen foods business in Europe, for roughly $2.9 billion. Nomad financed the acquisition with cash from its IPO, debt, and an additional $750 million of equity. Nomad intends to use Iglo as an "anchor investment" and base for future industry acquisitions.

Nomad's stock began trading near $10 and jumped to over $22 in mid-2015. Since then the stock has fallen to a low of $6.50 in 2016, presenting investors who want to be invested with Martin E. Franklin an opportunity to do so at a steeply discounted price. The stock has since rebounded to $12.

The wild price fluctuations in Platform Specialty Products and Nomad Foods are examples of why the public stock market can be such a rewarding place to invest if you are patient and disciplined. As I write this, an investor can purchase stock in Platform Specialty Products at a price below where Martin E. Franklin and Bill Ackman purchased them three years ago.

Platform and Nomad's stock prices rose too much, too fast as platform companies were in vogue. As platform companies became out-of-favor, the stock prices collapsed, but fell far below their intrinsic value.

At only fifty-two years old, Martin E. Franklin is the one investor profiled in this book whose best days are likely still ahead of him.

Below are some paraphrased highlights from my conversation with Martin E. Franklin.

Q. Have any investors had a big impact on you?
A. Marvin Schwartz of Neuberger Berman. He has an incredible instinct for value investing. He is also a well-mannered and fantastic person.

Q. Why start platform companies instead of a diversified holding company like Berkshire Hathaway or Koch Industries?
A. My personal holdings do consist of a few companies in different industries, much like a holding company, but when I raise capital to start platform companies they are an easier sell when they are pure plays in one industry.

Q. Why start "blank check" publicly traded companies instead of private equity companies?
A. (1) There is essentially infinite capital available in public markets. (2) You get the capital upfront. (3) The capital is inexpensive.

Q. If someone is to employ your strategy, how do they improve the odds of executing well?
A. (1) Become a good listener. (2) You need to surround yourself with people who know more about the subject than you do. (3) Be flexible in your thinking. (4) Be decisive.

Q. Leverage can be dangerous, but it also maximizes returns. What levels of leverage do you target?
A. Leverage can get you into trouble. We don't use excessive debt. We look to have a leverage ratio of three to four.

Q. What do you look for when making investments?
A. I have five core principles and I've done well when I've stuck to them. (1) The company must have a market leading niche. (2) It must have an identifiable moat. (3) There must be strong management in place. (4) There must be a history of strong, free cash flow. (5) It must have an attractive multiple.

Forever Investor: Michael Steinhardt (Strategy: Start-ups)

Michael Steinhardt is known for his legendary hedge fund, which achieved returns that earn him a spot in the money manager Hall of Fame. An investor who put $10,000 into his fund at inception in July 1967 would have had over $1 million after twenty years. That is an annualized return of 27 percent, net of fees.[17]

His hedge fund would move in and out of positions, looking for quick 10 percent or 15 percent gains and move on. The fund had an astounding annual turnover of 500 percent to 1000 percent.

Like Benjamin Graham, Steinhardt's best investment was a *forever investment* and a deviation from his investment style—proving again the importance of being flexible. In 2004, Steinhardt and Jono Steinberg invested a combined $9 million into WisdomTree, a company that manages ETFs; it was the company's entire market capitalization at the time. Steinhardt bought into the company at pennies a share and in mid-2015 the stock hit $25 a share.

The stock has been volatile and had a few severe declines from its highs, but Steinhardt has remained one of the largest shareholders. Steinhardt reportedly earned more from this one investment than from twenty-eight years of running one of the best-performing hedge funds to ever exist.[18]

Forever Investor: Steven Rales and Mitchell Rales (Strategy: Platform Companies)

Steven and Mitchell Rales got the last laugh over a *Forbes* author that mocked their youth in a 1985 article calling them "Raiders in Short Pants" and "cocky to the point of foolishness."

The multibillionaire brothers cofounded Danaher in 1983. They each own roughly 6 percent of the company, putting their respective holdings near $4 billion.

56

Until 1984 all operations had been in real estate, but that year the holding company acquired two new subsidiaries: Mohawk Rubber Company, a tire manufacturer, and Master Shield, a manufacturer and distributor of vinyl building products. Over the next two years, Danaher went on a buying spree, acquiring another twelve companies and became listed as a Fortune 500 company. Revenues climbed from $300 million in 1984 to $456 million by 1986. The fourteen subsidiaries were grouped into four business units: instruments, transportation, precision components, and extruded products.

The Rales brothers excel in fighting competition, divestment of unprofitable businesses, consolidation of facilities, and cost reduction. Much like private equity investors, Danaher developed a strategy of acquisition that was centered on the purchase of high-quality companies, but were underperforming and could be improved. It uses a management process called *kaizen*, which is based on the Toyota Production System and continually evaluates the manufacturing floor to identify and eliminate inefficiencies. Danaher takes it beyond the production process and requires sales and corporate staff to identify ways to improve quality and reduce costs.

Danaher recently acquired Pall for $13.6 billion and has split itself into two companies. Danaher is now a sciences company with businesses in diagnostics, water treatment, dental and life sciences with $16.5 billion in annual revenue. The other piece of Danaher, called Fortive Corp., is a conglomerate of industrial specialists. Fortive is expected to have annual revenue of roughly $6 billion and a free cash flow profile that will make it more of a dividend and buyback-oriented stock, even if acquisitions are also part of its strategy.

Colfax is another company founded by the Rales brothers. It is an industrial manufacturing and engineering company that provides gas and fluid-handling, and fabrication technology products and services. Colfax began trading at around $20 in May 2008. The stock reached a high of $75 in mid-2014 but has declined back to $20 due to a challenging operating environment in energy, emerging markets, and currency headwinds. With the track record of the Rales brothers, it would not be surprising if

Colfax grows rapidly through acquisitions over the next two decades.

Forever Investor: John Malone (Strategy: Platform Companies)

In 1973, John Malone took a job running TCI, the fourth largest cable operator in the country at the time. He was a mere thirty-two years old and TCI was in terrible shape. It had revenue of $19 million and a tremendous debt burden of $130 million. Moreover, TCI needed to continue to borrow more money to grow and expand.

Malone was taking a big risk by accepting the job at TCI. If TCI went bankrupt he'd not only lose his job, but it would be a permanent blemish on his resume. However, he believed if he could keep TCI's debt manageable and grow the business, he could make a fortune through stock options and stock purchases.

Immediately after starting at TCI things started to go poorly. The stock market started crashing in 1973, with the S&P 500 declining by -17.37 percent in 1973 and -29.72 percent in 1974. Interest rates also shot up to around 11 percent, making it significantly more costly to borrow money. With new regulations and price increases from suppliers, costs of expanding were rising fast. By the end of 1974 TCI had debt of $150 million, interest payments of $12 million, yet revenue was only $34 million.

In his first five years, Malone spent much of his time negotiating with bankers about debt covenants and extending the time periods for principal payments. If TCI defaulted on one of its interest payments, creditors could take over the company, and TCI became dangerously close.

When Malone joined TCI, he took out a loan to purchase stock. At the time the stock was at $7 and within his first year the stock fell below $1, making John Malone bankrupt on paper. Luckily he took a loan from a bank and there was not a margin call.

With TCI's stock around $1 in 1974 and 1975, two large shareholders wanted to sell and TCI feared a raider could buy the shares and take control. Debt covenants prevented TCI from repurchasing its own shares, so Malone and founder Bob Magness created a holding company in the name of Magness's dog, Tiger—avoiding a violation of the debt covenants. Over the next few years, Tiger Incorporated owned nearly one-third of the company's shares. Eventually they transferred ownership of Tiger Incorporated to a friend, with the option for TCI to buy it for $1000, which TCI later exercised.

Around 1976, TCI began to meet financial projections with regularity, which gave creditors some comfort. However, TCI was still reporting losses. Cash flow was strong though. Malone persuaded Wall Street to stop focusing on net income, which resulted in high taxes, and focus on cash flow. He brought it to their attention that TCI could expand at strong rates for a very long time through cash flow generation, without ever paying taxes because of interest expense, depreciation and amortization. In other words, high debt was not a burden for TCI; it saved them from paying taxes and fueled growth.

Around this time there was a boom in cable content (i.e., shows and programs). The Big Three networks (ABC, NBC, CBS) earned their revenue from advertising, while cable content providers earned their revenue from both the number of subscribers they are exposed to and advertising. In other words, the content providers relied on subscriber growth. Malone keenly observed that if TCI acquired ownership in content providers not already on TCI, he could make them more valuable if TCI carries them. It is the same strategy that Andrew Carnegie and railroad executives used when investing into the Pullman cars that relied on railroads for business.

Malone's first investment into cable content became a huge success: Black Entertainment Television (BET). The founder of BET needed $500,000 to get started. Malone said TCI would give BET $500,000, with $180,000 of that money being for 20 percent equity in BET and the rest being a loan.

A few years later, Discover was days away from bankruptcy when it caught Malone's interest. TCI bought 10 percent of the company for $6 million and eventually increased it to a 49 percent stake. TCI then bought stakes in the parent company of the Family Channel, AMC, and regional sports channels.

By 1981, TCI had two million viewers and was the largest cable company in the country. At the time cable companies were viewed as local monopolies because there was typically only one cable company in a town to choose from; however, they were closely regulated and wiring a city was very expensive. Cable companies had massive debt and big expansion plans, so customer service was at the bottom of the list, and the only thing a subscriber could do in protest was cancel his or her cable.

After nearly thirty years of building, cable was in only 19 percent of homes in 1978; over the next six years it doubled to 40 percent. Cable content providers also expanded from eight in 1978 to forty-seven in 1984. From 1976 to 1987, revenue of cable operators expanded from $900 million to $12 billion.

TCI became an investment vehicle as much as a cable company. From 1984 to 1987, Malone spent almost $3 billion for more than 150 cable companies. He took a $125 million stake in Turner Broadcasting that was worth $6 billion at its peak thirteen years later.

Malone, fearing government antitrust pressure, decided to spin-off the programming assets into a company called Liberty Media. When the company went public in 1991, it took off. In two years the stock went from $256 to $3700, resulting in Malone's personal investment of $42.1 million growing to more than $600 million.

TCI was later sold to AT&T in 1999, increasing Malone's net worth to $5 billion at the market peak. Malone maintained control over Liberty Media. He is a large investor and the chairman of both Liberty Media and Liberty Global (an international cable provider). His net worth was estimated at $12 billion at the end of 2015.

Forever Investor: Chuck Akre (Strategy: Four Filters)

Chuck Akre is unique among the list of forever investors because he operates a mutual fund. Managers of mutual funds have numerous disadvantages compared to the average investor or corporation: fickle investors who deposit or withdraw capital at the most inopportune times, restrictions on what percentage of a company it can own, and restrictions on how much it can initially invest into a company. Despite this, Akre has achieved one of the best track records among mutual funds and he earned his results with miniscule annual turnover of holdings.

Akre was heavily influenced by the investment classic *100-to-1 in the Stock Market* by Thomas Phelps, which told readers to look for companies that can compounded at high rates over long periods of time. Akre describes his investment approach as a three-legged stool, which is similar to Buffett's Four Filters. Akre looks for companies with (1) an extraordinary business model, (2) exceptional people, and (3) abundant reinvestment opportunities. By "reinvestment opportunities" he means being able to reinvest free cash flow back into the business at high rates of return, repurchase shares when undervalued, and make successful acquisitions.

In 1998, $10,000 invested into the Focused Fund Akre managed would have been $35,000 by the end of 2008 (it would have been over $55,000 in 2007 before the market decline). Over that same time period, $10,000 invested into the Russell 3000 would have returned a little more than $14,000.

Akre started his own fund in 2009, which by the end of 2015 has earned 15.57 percent annual returns, compared to 13.96 percent annual returns in the S&P 500. The fund, which had over $4.5 billion in assets at the end of 2015, has consistently produced returns remarkably close to the S&P 500 in every year, despite having a concentrated portfolio.

If you examine Akre's holdings in 2000 you will see that two of the top four positions were Markel and American Tower, which remain two of his largest positions today. CarMax and O'Reilly Automotive were also owned by him in the early 2000s and are still large holdings of his fund today. He is one of the very few money managers who is a forever investor.

Notes

1. John D. Rockefeller, *Random Reminiscences of Men and Events* (Creative English Publishing, 2013), 96.
2. Ibid., 13.
3. David Freeman Hawke, *John D. The Founding Father of the Rockefellers* (New York: Harper & Row, Publishers, Inc., 1980), 68.
4. Andrew Carnegie, *The Autobiography of Andrew Carnegie and the Gospel of Wealth* (New York: New American Library, a division of Penguin Group, 2006), 155.
5. Ibid., 73.
6. Harold C. Livesay, *Andrew Carnegie and the Rise of Big Business*, 3rd ed. (New York: Pearson Longman, 2007), 59.
7. David Cannadine, *Mellon: An American Life* (New York: Vintage Books, a division of Random House, Inc., 2006), 101.
8. Ibid., 118.
9. Ibid., 167.
10. Ibid., 139.
11. Benjamin Graham with commentary by Jason Zweig. *The Intelligent Investor*. Revised Edition 2006. First Collins Business Essentials.
12. Charles G. Koch, *The Science of Success: How Market-Based Management Built the World's Largest Private Company* (Hoboken, NJ: John Wiley & Sons, Inc., 2007), 10.
13. Daniel Schulman, *Sons of Wichita: How the Koch Brothers Became America's Most Powerful and Private Dynasty* (New York: Grand Central Publishing, a division of Hachette Book Group, Inc., 2014), 3.
14. Ibid., 77–78.
15. Ibid., 79.
16. Ibid., 142.
17. John Train, *The New Money Masters* (New York: Penguin Books, 1986), 31.

18. Michael Noer, "Michael Steinhardt, Wall Street's Greatest Trader, Is Back—And He's Reinventing Investing Again," *Forbes*, February 10, 2014 issue, http://www.forbes.com/sites/michaelnoer/2014/01/22/michael-steinhardt-wall-streets-greatest-trader-is-back-and-hes-reinventing-investing-again/3/#4d7411947c36.

Chapter Three

Quality of the
Business

The best businesses to buy are ones that you can own for decades and then your children can continue to own. A few of the most well-known examples are Chick-fil-A, Mars, Koch Industries, Ford, and Walmart.

Many great family-owned businesses prefer to stay private, rather than dealing with the Security and Exchange Commission, NYSE or NASDAQ, short-term shareholders, institutional investors, investment bankers, Wall Street analysts, short sellers, activist investors, and financial media. Taking all these into consideration, Charles Koch, CEO of Koch Industries, the second largest private company in the United States, said the company will be offered to the public "literally over my dead body."

An important consideration is that family businesses are more valuable forever investments to the controlling family than to passive investors. The reason for the difference is the value of being "owner operated." For example, you might be willing to buy a business that doesn't make any profits if it provides six-figure incomes for you, your spouse, your kids, and grandkids. There is value in the employment, not just the free cash flow.

Waterlox Coatings Corporation is a great example of a privately owned business that has provided impressive benefits to a family for 106 years. Waterlox is a fourth-generation owned company in Cleveland that makes premium wood finishes and competes against large corporations such as Sherwin Williams (Minwax) and Rustoleom (Watco), whose products are carried at big-box retailers Lowe's and Home Depot. Waterlox has been able to successfully compete with the big corporations for generations because it produces high-end niche products that many professional woodworkers endorse as the best products on the market.

Waterlox products are used largely on hardwood floors, but they are also designed for furniture and boats. These premium products are made from tung oil and a proprietary mix of resins. Tung oil is considered the best penetrating drying oil due to its unique ability to penetrate dense woods. Unlike linseed oil, Waterlox will not darken or yellow with age. Waterlox also penetrates deeper than urethanes and provides better below-the-surface protection. For these reasons, Waterlox appeals largely to the high-end market, where consumers are more concerned with quality than costs.

Due to hardwood flooring finishes being the primary source of revenue, one might infer that Waterlox sales would have declined substantially in the housing crisis of 2008–2009, but sales actually held up well. In its 106-year history, the company has endured World War I, the Great Depression, World War II, the Korean War, Vietnam War, two Gulf Wars, the Great Recession of 2008, and about a dozen other recessions. Despite frequent economic challenges, Waterlox has not experienced much cyclicality due to its niche-product nature.

The company also witnessed the emergence of e-commerce and the benefits and challenges it provided to the industry. CEO Jay Hawkins said in an interview that e-commerce has been almost entirely beneficial to Waterlox, allowing the company to reach customers that aren't located near a retailer who carries its products. He also credits the Internet for much better customer engagement. He said that prior to the Internet customers rarely reached out to ask questions about its products, but today the company stays busy answering phone calls and e-mails all day long.

Despite the success Waterlox has earned in the United States, only 10 percent of sales come from overseas. In an increasingly globalized consumer world, international sales may be a large opportunity for future generations.

While many companies with a controlling shareholder prefer to remain private, there are three good reasons to go public. One reason is that it is easier to raise capital as a public company. If your company is publicly traded it means you have met strict regulations and compliance standards, which may give investors a greater sense of ease. Investment bankers and investors are also more familiar with publicly traded companies than private companies, which may increase demand during rounds of capital raising. Publicly traded companies also have greater flexibility in how they raise equity or use it to pay for acquisitions.

Another important advantage of being publicly traded is that sometimes the public markets behave irrationally or overreact to news, creating rare opportunities to buy more shares at bargain prices. It is much rarer to find irrationally low prices for quality private businesses.

A third reason is the publicity and loyalty. If you are a publicly traded company, it gets you more media exposure. It also might create loyal customers as a result of loyal shareholders. If you're a shareholder of Lowe's and there is a Home Depot closer to your house, you might drive the few extra miles to Lowe's to support a company you are invested into.

Quality Businesses and Growth

The quality of a business is important, but so is growth. There are many high-quality businesses that are mature and struggle to grow. For example, Procter & Gamble and Johnson & Johnson are outstanding and predictable businesses, but have been struggling to grow revenue and earnings for the past decade. As forever investors we need both quality businesses and great long-term growth prospects.

Growth adds value and companies that trade at high multiples of sales, earnings, and book value can still be undervalued. In 2004, Google started trading at about $50 a share (adjusted for splits), which many considered a steep price at the time; Google earned roughly $30 a share in 2015. In 2004, Google looked expensive, but in reality it was dirt cheap at a forward P/E of 1.7 times 2015 earnings.

There are often high premiums paid for outstanding businesses, and opportunities to get them at attractive prices are very rare. However, a typical stock will fluctuate substantially from its high to its low each year. If an investor identifies companies he or she wants to own forever, there will likely be attractive prices to do so at some time.

Good Business	Poor Business
High Barriers to Entry	Obsolete technology
Brand Name	Money Loser
High ROIC	Weak Balance Sheet
Strong FCF	High Cost Producer
High Profit Margins	Commodity Product
Loyal Customers	Poor Corporate Governance

Growth Opportunity Through Acquisitions	High Capex Requirements
Responsible Management Team	Prone to litigation
Pricing Power	Heavy Regulation
Strong Balance Sheet	Fickle Customers
Asset Light	Low Margins
Low Capex Requirements	Losing Market Share
High-return Reinvestment Opportunities	
More Efficient than Peers	
Strong Organic Growth	
Gaining Market Share	
Growing Industry	

Quantitative Measures of a Business

Organic Growth of Sales, Profit, and Free Cash Flow

Investors want to own companies that are increasing in intrinsic value over time, therefore growth of sales, profit, and free cash flow are important measures of a business. Consistent growth for a mid- or large cap is often a sign of a good business with competitive advantages; however, the rate of growth over time is more important than consistency of growth.

Would you rather have 10 percent compounded annual growth over ten years or 15 percent annual growth over ten years? That sounds like a silly question. However, when companies have consistent 10 percent growth year after year, they often sell at high valuations than a faster growing company with less consistent annual growth. Forever investors can occasionally find buying opportunities into great companies who have uneven short-term growth.

Return on Invested Capital

High returns on invested capital and stable market share might provide quantitative evidence that a business has competitive advantages. High returns could not persist without a durable competitive advantage because new entrants would come into the market and compete away excess returns. A caveat, however, is that as analysts we only have access to historical returns on invested capital, which means we are only capable of analyzing historical competitive advantages from our data. We must look at other information to make estimates about the future returns on invested capital.

The best business to own is one that earns high returns on invested capital and can reinvest all of its free cash flow back into the business. If a company generates $1 billion in free cash flow a year, maintains a 15 percent return on invested capital, and can reinvest all that cash back into the business, it should continue to grow free cash flow by 15 percent a year. Unfortunately, most companies that earn high returns on invested capital cannot find opportunities to reinvest free cash flow back into the business.

The second-best business to own is one that earns high returns on invested capital and can't reinvest its cash flow back into the business, but management uses the cash wisely for acquisitions and opportune share repurchases.

Capital Expenditures (Capex)

When capital expenditures are as high as operating cash flow, it is an obvious sign of a poor business. If a company spends all of its cash flow to maintain its competitive position and does not develop sales and cash flow, then the owners are receiving no growth and no distributions of free cash flow. In other words, the owners are not receiving any benefits of owning the business. Therefore it is important to distinguish if capex is being used to maintain the competitive position or if it is for growth.

Capital expenditures for organic growth can be an attractive characteristic if the return-on-investment is high. For example, a rapidly expanding retailer will use all of its free cash flow on building more stores, which shows up as capex. New stores results in higher revenue, higher operating cash flow, better prices from suppliers, logistical advantages from scale, and so on.

An analyst can make reasonable assumptions from the change in revenue to determine if capex is for growth or not. If all free cash flow is being used on capex and revenue is not increasing, then the company is using it for maintaining its current business, not expanding. If, however, revenue is growing rapidly, then capex is likely being used for growth.

Balance Sheet

The quality of the balance sheet gives indicators about the quality of the business. It is important for investors to examine how the company raises capital. A company with a lot of debt may be expanding too aggressively or it may be a poor business that doesn't generate enough free cash flow to fuel expansion. If the debt is building up over time and management is issuing dividends, it is fair to conclude that management is thinking short-term and plans to leave the debt burdens to the next management team.

The intelligent investor should watch the corporate bonds in the secondary market to determine the riskiness of the balance sheet. Bond holders pay close attention to a company's financial solvency and when bond prices are falling, you should thoroughly examine why it is happening. Is it general market conditions, company specific conditions, or both?

Investors should also keep an eye on preferred shares. When a company issues preferred shares at high interest rates, it is often a sign that the company has exhausted its option in the debt market, and creditors view it as risky.

Qualitative Measures of a Business

Culture

Culture is of critical importance to a business, yet it is often overlooked by investors. There are many different cultures that can succeed depending on the type of industry. For example, an investment banking firm, a tech start-up, and a hospital will all have different cultures. What is important, however, is that the culture is one where employees believe in the greatness of the company and are highly motivated. One can draw meaningful inferences about a company's culture from the quality of its employees, satisfaction of its employees, and customer service. (We discuss the quality of employees in our chapter on management.)

Customer Service

Companies that are known for having the best customer service in an industry usually have strong management, happy employees, and loyal customers. Publications put out lists of the "most admired" and "most disliked" companies on an annual basis. The "most admired" companies usually hold themselves to a high ethical standard or are known for their customer service. The companies known for poor customer service, such as cable companies, are often the most disliked companies. If a company has the best product and terrible customer service, it will lose to the competition with better customer service.

Marketing and Sales

Marketing and sales has the same implications as customer service. The company with the best product will have difficulty beating the competition if it has inferior marketing and sales. Highly competitive businesses are especially dependent on marketing and sales. For example, what separates one investment advisor from another? What separates one insurance company from another? They all essentially sell the same product, but some advisors and insurance companies do better than others. The ones that succeed are often the ones that are the best at marketing, sales, and customer service.

Competitive Advantages

Competitive advantages are characteristic of most great businesses, but they alone do not make a business great. What good would it do to have monopoly rights to a drug that nobody needs or is impossible to produce at a profit? Competitive advantages in a great business, however, can make that business steady, safe, predictable, and highly profitable.

The past few years have reminded investors why durable competitive advantages are so important. Commodities are inputs for many products and the prices of commodities have fallen substantially in recent years. While companies with strong competitive advantages can keep prices level and profits will increase through lower costs of inputs, companies without competitive advantages are facing a much tougher reality. These highly competitive businesses are lowering prices in order to gain market share, which has resulted in declining revenue and profits in many businesses because the cost savings is being transferred to the customer.

It is important to recognize that competitive advantages can last a very long time, but they cannot last forever. A dominant local newspaper was once the prime example of an impenetrable competitive advantage; however, the Internet-created unforeseen competition and local newspapers have become far less profitable. McDonald's has had competitive advantages in the fast food industry for decades, but with a consumer shift toward healthier foods, those competitive advantages may vanish. The durability of the competitive advantage is more important than the size of the competitive advantage.

There are two common areas of competitive advantage: (1) Demand: switching costs, product differentiation, brand loyalty and (2) Supply: low-cost provider, niche products, and economies of scale.

Summary

What type of business should you want to own in a *declining market*? A great business that will increase in intrinsic value.

What type of business should you want to own in a *flat market*? A great business that will increase in intrinsic value.

What type of business should you want to own in a *rising market*? A great business that will increase in intrinsic value.

Chapter Four

Management

Would you rather own a company with outstanding management or poor management? That seems like an absurd question because everyone should want exceptional managers to run their companies; however, many investors don't place much emphasis on management, because they believe that if the management was hired, they must be qualified.

Businesses do not make decisions, people at the businesses do. As an owner of businesses, it is imperative that you are familiar with the people running the business.

The differences between failure, mediocrity, and wild success for a business often comes down to management. Even the best businesses won't thrive without talented management; however, the quality management is even more vital in highly competitive businesses.

For example, McDonald's and Burger King both have similar menu items, yet very different histories and operating performance. The difference between Best Buy and Circuit City, or Barnes & Noble and Borders, also came down to management. The difference between Amazon and all the other online bookstores in the early 2000s was Jeff Bezos. Starbucks also became wildly successful because of Howard Schultz, while all other coffee shops struggled to be profitable and expand.

Great managers come in all different shapes and sizes. There are some CEOs who are the nicest people you will ever meet, and then there are some CEOs who rely on their personality as a form of birth control. An outstanding CEO might be arrogant, extroverted, overweight, and smoke cigars, while another equally great CEO might be humble, introverted, and a self-disciplined health fanatic. We tend to be biased toward people who have qualities we admire or are similar to us, but the people we like are not necessarily the people who get results.

Leadership books tell readers what personality and character traits managers "should" have, but in reality things are not so well-defined and objective. Management consultants, business-school professors, and researchers are often overzealous in their attempts to quantify everything and use checklists. To them, everything has to be measured and fit nicely into a model they can publish in an academic journal or teach.

The greatest challenge with determining the quality of management is that it is forward looking. There are methods to measure a CEO's track record, but it is very difficult to judge what he or she will do in the future.

When assessing management's track record, examining how performance was driven is just as important as growth in sales, earnings, and free cash flow. An extreme example is financial companies prior to 2008. Many financial companies were growing rapidly up until 2008, but some of the growth came from taking on risks and being highly leverage. What appeared to be strong growth and talented management, was in fact carelessness and risk-taking.

Many people believe that because you cannot quantitatively identify talented management, it is impossible to tell which managers are talented. But that is like saying since you cannot quantify what makes a woman beautiful, you cannot identify beautiful women. You know one when you see one.

When evaluating management you must give considerable weight to both quantitative and qualitative measures.

Qualitative Measures of Management

Making qualitative judgments about executives requires the same approach as that of a manager responsible for hiring. There is not a definitive quantitative way to measure who you should hire; you have to learn as much about the candidate's experience and qualifications as possible, but also his or her personality, character, goals, and belief system. Intuition also plays a role. When making assessments of management teams, there are a few key areas of importance: long-term focus, culture, integrity, innovation, competitive advantages, and hiring.

Long-Term Focus. The most important quality when looking at management is a focus on long-term results, not short-term performance. Management should think and behave like a forever investor, not a short-term investor for a long time. Great managers will sacrifice smoothness of earnings if it means higher long-term returns. Does management make decisions based on meeting annual earnings expectations in an effort to boost the near-term stock price?

Culture. The culture of the company is also very important. Amazon was not content with just being an online bookstore. Google is not content with only being a search engine. Goldman Sachs and Blackstone attract some of the brightest and most talented people in finance due to their prestige and culture. Steve Jobs created an incredible culture at Apple.

Integrity. Companies do not think or act, people at companies do. If you are investing into private businesses you probably won't invest into a company managed by someone you don't trust. Likewise, you shouldn't invest into public companies with management that you do not trust. Do short-sellers, employees, suppliers, or competitors question management's ethics or integrity?

Innovation. Innovation is also a hallmark of talented management. Steve Jobs is the most ubiquitous example, but so are companies such as 3M, Disney, Starbucks, and Under Armour.

Competitive advantages. Another sign of talented management is when the competitive advantages of a company increase. A company that is expanding market share organically, while profit margins are maintained, is doing something better than competitors.

Hiring. Great managers are also great at hiring. Steve Schwarzman and Peter Peterson demonstrated that you can build a competitive advantage through the quality of your employees. Peterson served as CEO of Lehman Brothers from 1973–1984, and Schwarzman was the head of mergers and acquisitions. In 1985, the two partnered in founding Blackstone Group, which provided advisory services for mergers and acquisitions.

When Peter Peterson and Steve Schwarzman started Blackstone they had no track record in private equity investing. They wanted to raise a $1 billion fund and sent out 488 letters to contacts and previous clients. All they got back were a few notes that said "congratulations on the new business." The two spent a year crisscrossing the country only to yield a single $25 million investment from New York Life. Peterson and Schwarzman then came up with eighteen investors they thought would be strong candidates and all of them rejected Blackstone.

After a year of massive rejection, no track record in private equity, and a mere $25 million investment, they didn't give up.[1] In the second year of fundraising Prudential invested $100 million to be the lead investor, with tough terms. With a big name like Prudential as the anchor investor, Peterson and Schwarzman went to Japan and raised $175 million from financial companies that wanted to get involved in private equity. Then GE put in $35 million. GM rejected meeting with Blackstone several times until a First Boston banker used a church connection to get Blackstone access to GM; GM invested $100 million. Other pension funds put in $10 million to $25 million each after GM committed. They ended up raising $635 million for their first fund.[2]

Peterson and Schwarzman knew that they needed to hire people with experience in private equity if they were going to succeed. But they didn't want to just hire people with experience, they wanted the best people. In an interview in 2014 with Stanford Business School, Schwarzman said:

> ...if you attract 10s they'll always make it rain...they just have an ability to sense problems, design solutions, do new things...that's what a 10 does. A 9 is great at executing, can come up with good strategies, but not great strategies...a firm full of 9s, that's a winning firm. 8s, they just sort of do stuff that you tell them. And 7s and below...I don't know what they are since we don't tolerate them. It doesn't work in our industry. We are in the constant intellectual capital building business. Forget that we're called money managers or whatever else you want to call us, that's really our business.[3]

Today Blackstone is the world's largest alternative asset manager with over $300 billion in assets under management.

Google is another company that firmly believes the quality of its employees gives it a competitive advantage. Former CEO Eric Schmidt and Jonathan Rosenberg, manager of design and development, said that hiring is the most important thing for a manager to do. In their book, *How Google Works*, they say Google attracts the best and brightest people because of the "herd effect," which means passionate and brilliant people who get results want to work with other passionate and brilliant people who get results. Once you hire mediocre managers, those managers will hire mediocre employees. Soon you'll be stuck with a company full of mediocre workers.

While I would like to give credit to modern managers and the "attraction-selection-attrition model" for this observation, King Solomon said it much earlier in Proverbs 22:29: "Do you see any truly competent workers? They will serve kings rather than working for ordinary people."

Quantitative Measures of Management

Quantitative measures may be indicators of outstanding management or they may be indicators of an outstanding business. Quantitative data alone tells us about the strength of the business, but comparing a company's quantitative data to its peers gives us information about whether industry conditions are driving growth or if management is fueling it.

Another comparison method is to measure the company's market share in its industry. Is the company gaining on competitors or is it losing market share? Is it gaining market share by lowering its profit margins?

A frequently used quantitative measure used in the media is the stock price change under the CEO's tenure, but that alone is a poor measure because a CEO can inherit an overvalued or undervalued stock, prosperous or tough industry conditions, a strong or weak balance sheet, and strong operations or operational challenges. In other words, many CEOs get the credit or the blame for short-term conditions that are outside of their control. Rather than looking at the stock price, investors should start by looking at how much intrinsic value increased over management's tenure relative to peers. This can be measured by the increase in revenue per share, earnings per share, free cash flow per share, and book value per share.

Two financial statement metrics often used to identify talented management are profit margins and return on invested capital. However, viewing these metrics by themselves give us more information about the quality of the business, not the quality of management. Investors must compare a company to its peers to gain more insight. When a business has superior profit margins and return on invested capital relative to peers, or if there is a significant change under management's tenure, we might be able to make inferences about the quality of management.

How management uses free cash flow is also a measure of management talent and *The Outsiders: Eight Unconventional CEOs and Their Radically Rational Blueprint for Success* by William Thorndike makes a compelling case for investing into businesses with CEOs who are outstanding at allocating capital. The best business is one that can retain all of its free cash flow and reinvest it into operations at a high return on invested capital. The second-best option for a long-term business owner is to have management which makes acquisitions that increase intrinsic value and strengthen the company's competitive position. Repurchasing company stock is also a popular option and may increase shareholder value, but only if it is done when the stock is selling below its intrinsic value. Depending on the company's balance sheet, earning power, and interest rates on debt, reducing debt may be the best place to spend cash flow. The least attractive way to spend cash flow is to issue dividends to shareholders so they can reinvest the money after paying taxes on the distribution.

As an investor, you must examine management's record on capital allocation. Does management repurchase shares when the company is clearly undervalued or do they repurchase shares at any price? Have they made foolish acquisitions by overpaying for businesses with mediocre prospects? What is the return on retained earnings? Does the company issue dividends while debt is growing?

Corporate Capital Allocation

Management needs to do two things well to be successful: operate the business and deploy the cash flow generated by those operations. Many CEOs get hired because they are capable at operating the business; however, many are lacking in their ability to effectively deploy capital. Two companies with the same operating results will have very different outcomes for shareholders based on their ability to deploy capital.

In his 1987 letter to Berkshire Hathaway shareholders, Warren Buffett made this observation: "the heads of many companies are not skilled in capital allocation, and…it is not surprising because most bosses rise to the top because they have excelled in an area such as marketing, production, engineering, administration or, sometimes, institutional politics."

Companies only have three options for raising capital: debt, equity, or using internal cash flow. In all three of these options the calculation of the trade-off is straightforward: Is the return on the investment higher than the cost of capital? With cost of capital being zero for cash, companies can increase intrinsic value by deploying cash flow wisely.

Companies have five options for deploying capital and this is one of the most important management duties:

- Repurchase company common stock.
- Acquire ownership in other companies.
- Invest into current operations, new projects, research, and development.
- Reduce debt.
- Pay dividends to shareholders.

Dividends

While there are a certain segment of investors who love dividends, or even rely on dividends for income in retirement, dividends should be a last resort for management in the capital allocation process.

Dividends are the least tax-efficient capital allocation policy. By distributing free cash flow to shareholders through dividends, up to 20 percent of that cash is immediately lost through federal taxes. Depending on your state, you might also have to pay state taxes on your dividend income.

Let's go through the math. A company makes $1 billion dollars and pays a tax rate of 40 percent. The $600 million left after taxes is distributed to shareholders who pay 20 percent in taxes on that money, which leaves investors with $480 million. In other words, the government essentially owns 52 percent of this business since it gets 52 percent of the profits.

Contrast this with companies run by legendary cable CEO John Malone, who focuses on reducing tax liability to zero. John Malone's businesses have predictable cash flow and therefore can carry heavy debt, which results in high interest expense. He also frequently makes large acquisitions that result in depreciation and amortization. John Malone's companies usually report no profits, but generate strong free cash flow that is distributed to shareholders through share buybacks. John Malone has built himself a fortune estimated at $12 billion in the cable and media industry using this tax-efficient capital allocation strategy.

Jeff Bezos is another example of tax-efficient wealth creation. Amazon focuses on increasing revenue and market share, not profits. Amazon rarely reports a profit and hardly pays any taxes relative to its size, yet Jeff Bezos has built a fortune near $50 billion. Sometimes profits are overrated.

John Malone and Jeff Bezos are not the norm in corporate America, they are the exceptions. They recognize that taxes are by far the largest destroyer of wealth to shareholders. Malone and Bezos have the opposite strategy of the typical CEO who tries to maximize GAAP net income and then pays out much of the earnings in the form of dividends.

Given the tax-inefficiency of dividends, the decision to pay dividends should be the last resort after all other options have been exhausted. Managements issue dividends to shareholders because they believe shareholders can reinvest the cash, after-tax, better than management can before-tax. In reality, more value would likely be created if the company did not distribute the cash dividends and reinvested it into bonds or an S&P 500 index fund.

As discussed further in the chapter on "Six Types of Common Stock Investments," one of the most mind-boggling misuses of capital is when highly cyclical companies with heavy debt burdens pay dividends. Highly cyclical companies use dividends to "reward" shareholders and attract them to the stock; however, this is nothing more than a short-term gimmick that often backfires in industry troughs.

Consider an iron ore company that made huge profits when iron ore was above $100. The company had large capital expenditures and borrowed heavily to pay for them, yet issued dividends to shareholders. When iron ore prices collapsed, the share price fell over 90 percent from its high. Do long-term shareholders care about the dividends they received if the stock price falls 90 percent? Wouldn't retaining that dividend money and using it to reduce debt make more sense in the long-term?

If a company makes $1 billion in cash flow and spends $1.5 billion on capital expenditures, it should not be issuing a dividend. The company is essentially piling on debt to fund a dividend. This is very short-term thinking and puts many companies in bankruptcy, or on the verge, when industry conditions turn for the worse.

Share Repurchases

Earnings and free cash flow are not what ultimately drive the stock price; it is earnings per share and free cash flow per share that drive it. Share repurchases are a low-risk way of increasing per-share intrinsic value if repurchased when the stock is selling below its intrinsic value.

Share buybacks were uncommon a few decades ago, but today analysts and investors demand an "accelerated" stock buyback plan every time a stock falls 10 percent. Unfortunately, managers frequently give in. A company should not create a buyback program because the stock has fallen; it should only repurchase shares when the shares are (1) undervalued and (2) a more attractive capital allocation option than all other alternatives. Buybacks can destroy value if the company's stock price is far above intrinsic value; holding on to cash is better than paying $1.25 for $1.

Share repurchases were unconventional until the 1970s. Henry Singleton, CEO of Teledyne, was one of the pioneers of share repurchases and today still has one of the best track records for creating shareholder value through share repurchases. Singleton eventually led Teledyne to repurchase 90 percent of its own shares at bargain prices. Every management and finance student should be required to study Henry Singleton.

AutoZone is another excellent case study in how share buybacks can create tremendous shareholder value. From 2006 to 2015, revenue for AutoZone increased from roughly $6 billion to $10.2 billion. Net income during this time increased from roughly $570 million to $1.16 billion.

The stock price for AutoZone was at $100 in 2006, so what would you expect the price to be in 2015 after doubling net income? You'd probably expect the stock to be somewhere around double the 2006 price; however, in 2015 the stock was at $700 a share.

What drove AutoZone's stock to a seven-fold return in a decade when net income only doubled? It was smart share buybacks. From 2006 to 2015, the company reduced shares outstanding from 75 million to 32 million and earnings per share skyrocketed from approximately $7.60 to $36.80. Also, because management has been so successful at creating shareholder value, it is now given a higher P/E by investors today that it received in 2006. Unfortunately for current shareholders, a high P/E hurts a company that consistently repurchases large amounts of its own stock.

Acquisitions and Other Long-term Investments

While analysts forecast organic growth of companies, it is often acquisitions that are the largest drivers of growth. Organic growth is somewhat predictable for analysts, but acquisitions are entirely unpredictable. Therefore, the companies that are most likely to have a dislocation of value are companies that frequently make acquisitions.

With acquisitions being such a large part of a company's growth, it is important to measure management's talent at making them. Similar to stock repurchases, it is important to acknowledge that acquisitions can add value or destroy value depending on the price. Acquisitions are nothing more than investments and companies can overpay or get bargains on their investments.

While individual investors usually get all the fame for brilliant investments, some of the best investments are done by companies. Consider Yahoo's investment in Alibaba. Yahoo paid $1 billion for part ownership of Alibaba in 2005. In 2012, Yahoo made $4.6 billion by selling some of those shares back to Alibaba. Then, in 2014 Alibaba had an IPO and Yahoo still had a stake worth $35 billion at the time. In other words, a $1 billion investment in Alibaba turned into nearly $40 billion twelve years later. While Yahoo's business has struggled to grow, its investment into Alibaba made Yahoo's intrinsic value soar.

Many people are familiar with the Alibaba investment by Yahoo because returns like that are so rare; most acquisitions and investments don't turn out that way. While many acquisitions are successful, there are plenty that end up being poor investments.

A recent example of a poor investment is Hewlett Packard's acquisition of Autonomy in 2011 for $11.7 billion. Within a year HP wrote off $8.8 billion from the acquisition; however, the honors for worst acquisition in recent history may go to Bank of America. It paid $4 billion for Countrywide during the 2008 financial crisis. Since then losses from operations, legal expenses, and fines are estimated to be near $40 billion.[4] It is rare to lose ten times your money on an investment.

Cisco announced in September 2015 that it is making its 182nd acquisition, which demonstrates the importance of acquisitions to maintain or grow competitive positions. CEO John Chambers said that he knows based on the company's history that one-third of Cisco's acquisitions are going to fail, but he just doesn't know which ones.

Many of the best CEOs are talented at making acquisitions, but the size of the company also plays an important role. Apple, Google, and Microsoft are now so large that there are few acquisition opportunities that will have a meaningful impact on the companies' revenue and earnings.

Invest into Current Operations, New Projects, Research, and Development

The ideal use of cash flow is to reinvest it back into the business at a high return on capital invested; however, many businesses don't earn high returns on invested capital and the ones that do earn high returns usually have trouble finding ways to reinvest the money.

Investing cash flow back into current operations can be smart or foolish, depending on how the money is being used. An investor should expect to see an increase the company's competitive position, sales, and free cash flow if it is using its cash flow internally. If the money is being used to maintain the company's competitive position and it isn't resulting in an increase in sales and cash flow, then it is not a great business, but it still might be necessary to combat a further decrease in its operations.

An example of an industry that retains most of its cash flow is retail. Having one retail store usually doesn't make the owners well-off financially and is risky because the success is dependent on one location. If that one store starts to have sales and profit declines, the entire business is in danger.

If you are a retailer with a dozen locations, one store that is underperforming will have a lesser impact on the business. Expansion for a retailer can not only increase profits, it can reduce risks. Expansion, however, must be done with caution; borrowing too much, too quickly may put the company in jeopardy if there is a severe recession or fierce competition.

Reduce Debt

Companies use debt to finance projects, operations, and acquisitions. However, companies should consider reducing debt under certain circumstances.

One obvious reason to reduce debt is that it makes the balance sheet stronger, which can improve a company's credit rating and make future borrowing cheaper. Reducing high interest debt and taking on debt at a lower rate is one of the most efficient ways to cut costs.

Another reason to reduce debt is if the debt load is so high that interest expense is consuming a large percentage of the cash flow the company generates. Companies should also reduce debt if the interest rate on the debt is higher than the rate of return the company can get by investing the cash flow elsewhere.

Keep in mind that reducing debt gives you a *guaranteed* rate of return, while projects and acquisitions give you a *potential* return.

Control of Management

Many investors believe that having control of management is a way to reduce risk and increase shareholder value. These investors include corporations, entrepreneurs, activist investors, private equity firms, and venture capitalists. However, not every investor wants to be involved in management, nor does everyone have the expertise to make executive decisions.

If you do not have control of management, the best way to mitigate risk is by investing your money into companies that have management with integrity and exceptional talent. There are a handful of remarkable managers who know much more than anyone else about their business, phenomenally manage operations, and are outstanding at allocating capital. You couldn't replace these people with better management because they are as good as it gets. These are the managers we should be looking to invest with.

Notes

1. David Carey and John E. Morris, *King of Capital: The Remarkable Rise, Fall, and Rise Again of Steve Schwarzman and Blackstone* (New York: Crown Business, a division of Random House Inc., 2010), 51.
2. Ibid., 52–55.
3. *Blackstone's Stephen Schwarzman on Hiring Phenomenal People*, Stanford Business School, Published November 26, 2014, https://www.youtube.com/watch?v=3jGc8biSYHA.
4. Dan Fitzpatrick, "B of A's Bluder: $40 Billion-Plus," *Wall Street Journal Online*, July 1, 2012, http://www.wsj.com/articles/SB100014240527023035615045774953329478707736.

Chapter Five

When to Buy, How Much to Buy, and When to Sell

Your goal as an investor should be to simply purchase, at a rational price, a part interest in an easily understood business whose earnings are virtually certain to be materially higher, five, ten, and twenty years from now. Over time, you will find only a few companies that meet those standards—so when you see one that qualifies, you should buy a meaningful amount of stock.
—Warren Buffett, 1996 Berkshire Shareholder Letter

Bargain hunters look for companies that appear cheap, then they dig in and see if the companies are worth owning. By contrast, forever investors find companies that are worth owning (outstanding businesses with great management), then they wait for an attractive buying opportunity. In other words, bargain hunters focus first on price and second on the operations. Forever investors focus first on the operations and management. If the forever investor finds a business that looks promising, then he or she waits for a unique buying opportunity.

Patience is required for both approaches. For the bargain hunter, patience is required for the stock to reach its calculated intrinsic value so it can be sold. For the forever investor, patience is required to buy at an attractive price.

Price is always important no matter how great the business. Buying the best company with the best management can yield poor or mediocre results if the price is too high.

Bargain hunters are often near-sighted. They search for opportunities to buy businesses far below intrinsic value and sell them in a few years (or less) when the price approaches intrinsic value. The best forever investors, however, are both near-sighted and far-sighted. Forever investors search for businesses that are priced below intrinsic value, but they don't find it necessary to sell when it approaches intrinsic value because the intrinsic value is expected to continue to increase at a strong pace.

One of the most important things for an investor to do is be willing to be inactive if there are not attractive opportunities. It is also one of the hardest things for investors to do, especially for money managers. Too many investors are concerned about missing out on a rising market that they are always buying, no matter the market levels and prices of businesses. Never was this more evident in recent history than the speculative prices achieved during the late 1990s. Investing into a business, or the market, because you don't want to miss out on short-term returns is purely speculative.

The psychological challenge with forever investing is that people want immediate feedback. If you are a short-term investor, it doesn't take long for you to know if you were right or wrong. For a forever investor, it can take years for you to determine if you were right or wrong.

To the forever investor there is a strong correlation between the holding period and the success of a purchase. The quicker you sell something you've bought, the greater the mistake in purchasing it. The greatest purchases are ones you "buy well and never sell".

Valuing a Business

The intrinsic value of a company is not a precise figure because a company's past is not for sale; you are buying its future. It is easy to calculate the historical performance of a company, but to value a company you need to calculate the future operating results of the company. Since the future is not perfectly predictable, your determination of intrinsic value will also not be perfectly precise.

Your calculation of intrinsic value should be a range based on different scenarios. The most predictable and stable companies have a narrow range, while unpredictable companies have a wide range. Precise valuation is dishonest valuation.

Another reason precise valuation is not accurate, and why markets are not perfectly efficient, is because investors have different goals. For example, the discount rate has a large impact on a discounted cash flows valuation. If you use opportunity cost as your discount rate and it is 7 percent, but mine is 12 percent, we will come up with very different estimates of the company's present value. If an investor uses interest rates as the discount rate, such as a ten-year Treasury, a big move in interest rates can drastically change the value of discounted future cash flows. In other words, the only way valuation can be precise, and markets perfectly efficient, is if everyone uses the same discount rate and knows what the company will produce in free cash flow every year going forward.

Since valuation is not precise, we not only need a range of valuations based on different expectations, but we also need a "margin of safety" when making a purchase. When Benjamin Graham introduced the concept of margin of safety he recognized that valuation is not precise, there is uncertainty, and we are going to make mistakes.

There is an argument that it should be easier to predict a stock one to two years out than five years out because it is easier to predict near-term sales and earnings. It is true that it's easier to predict the immediate future with regard to sales and earnings, but it is impossible to predict short-term stock-price movements. In the long-term a stock price moves with intrinsic value; in the short term, a stock price moves with the whims of the market, supply/demand, and investor sentiment. In other words, even if you precisely predict what earnings and sales will be next year, you can still be very wrong about what happens to the price of the stock.

One rule of thumb during your analysis is that you shouldn't look at the price of a company before you attempt to value it. If you do, you will be biased toward the current market price. Many investors make the mistake of looking at the price, then deciding if the business is worth more or less.

However, there are still psychological pressures when calculating the value before looking at the price. If someone determines a business is worth approximately $100 million, but it is trading for $150 million, the person performing the valuation, searches for reasons to explain the $150 million price and might nudge the valuation up a little. Conversely, if it is determined a business is worth $100 million, but it is trading for $60 million, the person performing the valuation might think he or she is missing something important and nudges the valuation down or decides the business has too much uncertainty.

Calculating the price of a stock is much easier than estimating its value. There are only two ways to calculate the price of a stock. One way is to simply take the market cap or asking price. The second way is "enterprise value," which is the market cap plus net debt. Enterprise value is an important consideration. Imagine two identical companies earn $1 billion and trade at a market cap of $15 billion. If one has $5 billion in debt and the other no debt, obviously the debt-free company is cheaper.

Investing in common stocks is similar to investing in bonds. For a bond that is expected to make all of its payments, the value of the bond is equal to the present value of the maturity value plus coupon payments. For a stock, the value is the present value of all future free cash flow. If you don't want to own a bond to maturity, then you are speculating on short-term price movements. It is speculative to purchase a bond that matures in ten years just because you think it will perform well over the next two years. Similarly, it is speculative to value a company based on its entire future free cash flow, but buy it with the intention of selling it in two years.

Forever investors do not buy a stock just because it "should" go up 25 percent in the near term; they buy because they foresee an increase in intrinsic value that will make today's price look very cheap in ten years.

The intrinsic value of a company may or may not be based on earnings. For some companies the reported earnings significantly understate the value of the company and for others they significantly overstate the value. Cash flow and free cash flow are what really matter.

Amazon is a company that often reports negative earnings, but it is not a worthless company—it is also not easy to come up with a reasonable calculation of intrinsic value for Amazon. Liberty Global also consistently reports negative earnings but generates strong and predictable free cash flow. Berkshire Hathaway has erratic and unpredictable earnings and free cash flow, therefore book value is a better measure of intrinsic value for Berkshire.

The valuation method I am least fond of is that of "relative value." This is a favorite of investment bankers and private equity companies. Relative value is comparing the financial metrics of one company, such as EBITDA, to a similar company. For example, if one company is at ten times EBITDA, they might say that a similar company at eight times EBITDA is undervalued.

Comparing metrics and prices can be useful, but don't confuse prices with valuation. If one company is overvalued and a similar company is slightly less overvalued, it doesn't mean the slightly less overvalued company is cheap. Investment bankers and private equity firms use this method to try to find out what the company "should" trade for in the market (i.e., price), not its valuation. Don't confuse price and valuation.

How to Discover New Investment Opportunities

When talented and established investors speak to MBA students, one of the questions that inevitably comes up is how to search for attractive investments. The answers rarely satisfy students who are looking for a secret source of information to make the process easier. Unfortunately, there is no one source of opportunities—it is a grind.

Before you begin looking for opportunities you must learn accounting: it is the language of business. Anyone who doesn't have a good grasp on accounting issues will be prone to error and exposed to additional risks. Investors don't have to have an accounting degree, but they should be able to understand the footnotes in a company's 10-Q and 10-K.

While there is no one source for all ideas, drudging endlessly at every source may produce one or two ideas a year. However, there are good sources and poor sources and it is important to separate important information from "noise." There is continuous information from CNBC, Bloomberg, Fox Business, Twitter, Facebook, Yahoo Finance, and hundreds of websites devoted to investment news—and 99.9 percent of it is noise. What ultimately matters is not how much information you get, but how you process the information. Here are some of the areas of idea generation:

- Monitoring: The NASDAQ has approximately twenty-three hundred domestic companies and the NYSE has roughly eighteen hundred. After eliminating the poor businesses that lose money, companies you don't understand well (e.g., solar panels), and ones that are difficult to predict (e.g., steel), you are left with a few hundred of the best businesses in the United States. Study these companies closely and become an expert on each one. Wait for opportunities to pick up one to two a year at attractive prices.
- News: Read a plethora of magazines, newspapers, websites, and trade journals.
- Research: There are no substitutes for reading 10-Qs, 10-Ks, and conference call transcripts.
- Third-Party Reports: Read reports on roughly thirty-five hundred companies from Value Line and S&P Capital IQ.
- Like-Minded Investors: Read the SEC filings of other top investment managers with a similar investment philosophy to find companies that might not have been on your radar.
- Network: Ask doctors, scientists, engineers, bankers, and other specialists to keep you informed about new companies or old companies doing something new.
- Competitors: When you examine a company, look at all of its competitors.
- Corporate Change: An IPO, spin-off, major acquisition, or new CEO can increase uncertainty and cause a dislocation of value.
- Experience: As you become more experienced you will become well acquainted with most of the high-quality publicly traded companies.

Another favorite question that new investors have is whether they should focus on small caps, midcaps, or large caps. Small caps are where there should be the most inefficiencies in theory, but in reality there is an abundance of money in mutual funds and hedge funds chasing these investments. If you are looking for inefficiencies, you should look at micro caps and over-the-counter (OTC) stocks, which are usually shunned by mutual funds, ETFs, conservative investors, and large investors.

The challenge with micro caps is that they are usually not very good businesses. Very small companies typically don't have competitive advantages and strong market positions. They also usually don't attract talented management. Mid- and large cap companies usually have the strongest competitive advantages and attract the best and brightest managers.

Big companies can become too big though. If you are looking for a stock to go up five or ten times over the next decade, you shouldn't be investing in Apple or Google today at $500 billion market caps. If you want those types of returns you should look for companies below the $30 billion price range.

Without going into detail, below are some areas that have historically been a source of 10-baggers. Many 10-baggers also come from a combination of areas:

1. Buying near the low during market panics
2. Companies with strong competitive advantages and can reinvest cash flow at high rates of return
3. Management with a talent for being serial acquirers of businesses
4. Companies with rapid organic growth that exceeds expectations
5. Distressed situations or bankruptcy concerns
6. Highly cyclical companies at their trough
7. Companies that aggressively expand operations at the beginning of a booming period
8. Companies that repurchase large quantities of its own shares at depressed prices
9. Companies that develop a new product that is wildly successful
10. Companies that get a large new contract

When to Buy

Throughout this book we have discussed *what* to buy, but *when* to buy is equally important. There is not much to say about when to buy because it comes down to one thing: price. Even a great company is not a great investment if the price is too high.

Timing will always impact your performance. Great timing will make you look smarter than you are. Being right too soon, or poor timing, can be just as painful as being wrong. Anyone who purchased a business in 2007, right before the economic crisis, can relate.

Forever investors buy stocks as if the market were going to be closed for the next ten years. If the timing is unlucky, the forever investor will still make out OK over ten years if the company and management are great.

A forever investor must also have strong conviction in his or her investment decisions. Whenever anyone buys a company, someone else is selling that company. The seller is not trying to do anyone a favor, he or she thinks it is time to get out. There will always be others who disagree with you, and if you aren't convinced you should own the business forever, then you shouldn't buy it at all.

Diversification

I always tell the students in business school they'd be better off when they got out of business school to have a punch card with 20 punches on it. And every time they made an investment decision they used up one of those punches, because they aren't going to get 20 great ideas in their lifetime. They're going to get five, or three, or seven and you can get rich off five, or three, or seven. But what you can't get rich doing is trying to get one every day.

—Warren Buffett

The amount of proper diversification depends on the type of investor. Wide diversification makes the most sense for investors who don't know what they are doing. These investors should simply purchase a few index funds if they have a long-term time horizon. Investors also might want to follow a strategy similar to the Yale model and diversify into other asset classes. Yale's endowment fund has the following target asset allocation for 2016[1]:

Absolute Return: 21.5 percent
Leveraged Buyouts: 16.0 percent
Foreign Equity: 14.5 percent
Venture Capital: 14.0 percent
Real Estate: 13.0 percent
Natural Resources: 8.5 percent
Bonds and Cash: 8.5 percent
Domestic Equity: 4.0 percent

The Chief Investment Officer of Yale's endowment, David Swensen, is not an expert investor—he is an asset allocator. Since he started his job in 1985, his goal has been to find the most talented investors in each asset class and make long-term investments with those investors. Many other institutions and family offices have since adopted this model over the past few decades; however, it is not easy to replicate for the average investor because most top investors require large investments. Putting money with mediocre investors in any asset class is likely to produce disappointing results. A few other differences between the Yale model and the average investor is that Yale invests tax-free and expects to exist forever, therefore it doesn't have to worry about tax consequences, retirement, or estate planning.

While diversification has its merits, no one can be an expert at everything and it may be best to put all your money into your area of expertise. A talented real-estate investor may be best off having nearly his or her entire net worth in real estate. A talented forever investor is likely to be best off having most of his or her money in private and public businesses. An entrepreneur may be best off having his or her entire net worth in the company he or she runs. And a talented private equity investor should not necessarily buy publicly traded stocks, real estate, and bonds just for the sake of diversification.

The proper amount of diversification is also dependent on the type of investor. An insurance company that grows its float over time will have to approach diversification differently than an investor with a fixed amount of money and no capital inflows or outflows. When there are expected future capital inflows, the manager can be very concentrated in early years, keep those positions for very long time periods, and add new positions as more capital comes in. An investor with a fixed amount of capital must sell something if he or she wants to buy something new.

The forever investor has the goal of purchasing outstanding businesses and never selling them. These opportunities are rare and when the forever investor is presented with such an opportunity, it makes sense to make a large commitment. When you come across an opportunity that appears once or twice in a decade, you should purchase a meaningful amount. Putting only 5 percent of your money into the best idea you've ever come across makes little sense. Philip A. Fisher wrote that owning large quantity of stocks is usually not a sign of genius, but an indication the investor lacks conviction in his or her investments. Fisher also argues that an investor may get better results owning a handful of companies he or she knows and understands well, than owning a basket of companies that he or she knows little about.[2] Billionaire hedge-fund manager Stanley Druckenmiller echoed the same view as Philip A. Fisher:

> I think diversification and all the stuff they're teaching at business school today is probably the most misguided concept everywhere. And if you look at all the great investors who are as different as Warren Buffett, Carl Icahn, or Ken Langone, they tend to make very, very concentrated bets. They see something, they bet it, and they bet the ranch on it. And that's kind of the way my philosophy evolved...only maybe one or two times a year do you see something that really, really excites

you…The mistake I'd say 98 percent of money managers and individuals make is they feel like they got to be playing in a bunch of stuff. And if you really see a rare opportunity, put all your eggs in one basket, and then watch the basket very carefully.[3]

The weight you give to each investment matters more than the number of investments you make. A portfolio of one hundred stocks can be more concentrated than a portfolio of fifteen stocks. If you have one hundred investments and your top six ideas make up 80 percent of your assets, you are more concentrated than an investor who equally weights twenty-five stocks.

There are also many large corporations that are made up of dozens of businesses. When you own companies such as GE, Microsoft, Google, Disney, or Berkshire Hathaway, you may own one stock, but you are getting ownership into many businesses. An investor into these types of companies might be comfortable with three to ten holdings.

Probability trees are used to support wide diversification; however, probability trees are misleading because no one knows the true probability of future returns and risks. Probability theory says that if you buy enough companies with a fifty-fifty chance of tripling or going to zero, then it *guarantees* a healthy 50 percent return. However, if there is really an 85 percent chance the stock will go to zero, then the expected return is −55 percent. You can never know the probabilities of returns, and therefore probability trees are an exercise in futility.

The great risk of a concentrated portfolio is overconfidence in one's abilities. Many investors occasionally experience overconfidence until the market humbles them. It is essential to have confidence in your ability to make sound investment decisions, but it is equally important to remember that you are not infallible. To paraphrase Pastor Rick Warren, "Humility is not denying your strengths, it is acknowledging your weaknesses."

Cautious investors purchase a small amount of a stock out of fear something might go wrong, which also means they get small rewards if they are right. Your allocation into each company should be based on your conviction the company will earn strong long-term returns with a very small risk of permanently losing money. The higher the certainty and expected returns, the more money should be allocated to it. In other words, only you know the proper amount of diversification for yourself.

Managing Risk

> Eternal vigilance is the price of liberty.
> —Thomas Jefferson

Managing risk is important for any investment strategy, but it is especially important for investors with concentrated portfolios. An investor who only owns a few companies must have unwavering conviction that each company will produce positive long-term returns because, as any intelligent investor knows, it is far easier to prevent losses than to rectify them. A loss of 50 percent requires a 100 percent return to get back to even.

Two of the most important risk management concepts are the "circle of competence" and the "margin of safety."

In chapter one, we already discussed the circle of competence. However, keep in mind that one person can make a low-risk and sound forever investment in a company within his or her circle of competence; meanwhile someone else can purchase it on the same day and be gambling because it is not within that investor's circle of competence. For this reason "piggy-backing" on other investors' ideas is not a sound investment strategy. It makes sense to follow what other talented investors are doing to help find companies that might not have been on your radar, but you need to do your own disciplined analysis of the companies.

Also, you can make a low-risk and sound investment into a great company at one price, but it may be a high-risk investment at a higher price. A "margin of safety" is required no matter how great the company.

The concept of a margin of safety leads to a conclusion that is contrary to most thinking in finance. Investment theory states that high-risk investments must provide investors with a high expected return to compensate for the above-average risk. This conclusion is often true. For example, a company with a credit rating from Standard & Poor's of B will have to provide a higher yield to investors than a company with an AAA rating. However, this has led to the fallacy of circular reasoning. Many have misunderstood this relationship to mean that if you want to get higher returns, you must take more risk. If investing were that easy, everyone would own junk bonds and no one would own Treasuries. High risk usually means high losses, not high returns.

The margin of safety provides more practical thinking on the subject of risk and return for the investor. According to the margin of safety concept, if you buy a company at a significant discount to intrinsic value, your risk of losing money is low. Also, you have an opportunity for high returns since you are buying it at a steep discount to intrinsic value. Conversely, if you pay a price far above-intrinsic value, you are taking a higher risk and your opportunity for gain is lower.

In other words, it is nonsense to claim that you have to take high risks to earn high returns. The correct investment rule should be "the larger the discount to the present value of future cash flows, the lower the probability of loss and the higher the potential return."

Liquidity is an area of focus for money managers concerned about meeting investor redemptions, but for the typical investor liquidity should not be much of a concern. High liquidity can have psychological disadvantages before a purchase because you know that if the investment doesn't work out, you can sell it quickly. In other words, you may become less disciplined in your investment decisions because of how easy it is to get out and move on. It is better to make a great investment into something illiquid than make a poor or mediocre investment into something with high liquidity. That sounds like common sense, but you'd be surprised by how many people think high liquidity means less risk of losing money and low liquidity means higher risk of losing money.

To properly manage risks, investors also need a good grasp on accounting to be able to recognize "aggressive accounting." If short-sellers accuse a company of improper accounting, don't brush it off as someone shouting false allegations about the company to make money. It is wise to give it serious consideration and analysis. Short-sellers are often wrong when it comes to accounting accusations, but when they are right the stock can drop 80 percent or even go to zero. It is a very serious risk worth careful and thorough examination. For this reason, and others, integrity of management needs to be an important part of your investment process.

There are substantial risks in every company, with many of them listed in the 10-K under "Risks Related to Our Business." A few main ones include Company Risk, Industry Risk, Market Risk, Credit Risk, Currency Risk, Regulatory Risk, Inflation Risk, Macroeconomic Risk, Risk of Lawsuits, and Risk of Fraud or Corruption by employees. An intelligent investor never purchases ownership in a company without reading through this portion of the 10-K.

The greatest risk for an investor is uncertainty about the future. You can have all the information to make an informed and educated forecast about the future prospects of a company, but circumstances change. Therefore a forever investor must stick to only those investments which have a high degree of certainty. You may get zero or one idea a year in a normal market and half dozen ideas in a market panic when prices are irrationally low, but it is better to be patient than poorer.

Billionaire hedge-fund manager David Tepper has a saying around his office: "There are times to make money—and times to avoid losing money." When prices for businesses are at extreme levels, either low or high, you must act accordingly. It is better to underperform when businesses are at high prices than to chase short-term returns and lose money when prices revert to reasonable levels.

103

When to Sell a Business

> ...when we own portions of outstanding businesses with outstanding managements, our favorite holding period is forever.
> —Warren Buffett, 1988 Berkshire Hathaway Shareholders Letter

Throughout this book I've made a case for having a target holding period of forever. The word "target" has intentionally been emphasized. Businesses are not static, and there are circumstances where holding on to an investment no longer makes sense.

Before we get into when to sell a forever investment, let's first acknowledge the different types of investors and the strategic and psychological impact of each target holding period.

<u>Investor Type and Target Holding Period</u>
Trader: Hours to Weeks
Momentum Investor: Months
Bargain Hunter: One to Three Years
Buy-and-Hold Investor: Three to Five Years
Forever Investor: Forever

Much of Wall Street is comprised of traders and momentum investors. These investors are like bachelors who refuse to get into a serious relationship; for them, new is always better.

A trader has no regard for the quality of a business or the valuation; he or she is looking for a change in investor sentiment or technical analysis to cause a change in price. The momentum investor also has little regard for business fundamentals and valuation; he or she is looking for stocks that are in-favor.

Mutual funds and a large portion of individuals are either bargain hunters or buy-and-hold investors. Bargain hunters look for businesses they don't want to own forever, but they believe the company is undervalued. These are often slow-growers, asset plays, and turnarounds. Bargain hunters hold their nose at the valuations of stalwarts and growth companies. For a bargain hunter, a successful investment is one that increases in price quickly and then can be sold near its intrinsic value. Bargain hunters typically don't own companies for more than a few years. If he or she does, then the investment has remained below the investor's estimate of intrinsic value or the investor thinks intrinsic value will go up over time, which means the bargain hunter switched to a "Growth At a Reasonable Price" (GARP) approach.

Buy-and-hold investors have the patience to wait years for ideas to work out. They typically focus on cyclicals, stalwarts, growth companies, asset plays, and turnarounds. They tend to avoid slow growers unless it provides a high dividend. Private equity investors are considered buy-and-hold investors as well, but they often favor slow growers, then they cut expenses, make bolt-on acquisitions, and sell the company.

Lou Simpson, former Chief Investment Officer of GEICO, is an excellent buy-and-hold investor and uses a strategy similar to the Four Filters that Buffett and Munger employ. Simpson retired from GEICO a few years ago and now runs SQ Advisors out of Naples, Florida, which has already grown to more than $3 billion in assets under management. Buffett highlights Lou Simpson's investment record in the Berkshire Hathaway 2004 shareholder's letter, calling him "a synch to be inducted into the investment Hall of Fame." Over Simpson's first twenty-five years at GEICO, his investment performance in equities was 20.3 percent annual returns versus 13.5 percent annual returns in the S&P 500. His track record is an interesting study because you will notice that even the best investors have multiyear periods of underperformance.

Buy-and-hold investors correctly believe it is easier to predict what will happen to the fundamentals of a company over the next three to five years than over a ten-year or twenty-year period. While this may be true, it is extremely difficult to predict how the stock price will behave in a three- to five-year period. If a company has a P/E of seventeen and grows earnings 30 percent over a three-year period (9.14 percent annually), but the P/E falls to thirteen, the stock price will not have moved.

Long-term fundamentals are impossible to predict with a high degree of precision, but you can find companies that have an extremely high probability of growing intrinsic value at strong rates. If a company earns that same 9.14 percent annual growth of earnings over twenty years, and the P/E falls from seventeen to thirteen, the investor would still have earned an annual return of 7.7 percent. Time is the friend of a wonderful business—and wonderful investor.

Forever investors must be the most disciplined of any investors because they don't plan to sell the businesses they acquire. Opportunities to purchase businesses you want to own forever are rare, therefore forever investors tend have very concentrated portfolios. When you own a concentrated portfolio there is little room for error—if one company goes bankrupt or drops 80 percent, it will have a substantial negative impact on the performance of the portfolio.

Due to the heavy burden of mistakes, forever investors favor great companies with outstanding management; these are often stalwarts and growth companies. Forever investors wait for rare opportunities to buy when the price is very attractive and there is an obvious "margin-of-safety." Bargain hunters want to "buy low and sell high," while forever investors want to "buy well and never sell."

One of the hardest things to do in investing is to hold on to a stock after it has gone up and doesn't appear cheap anymore. Remember that you cannot have a stock go up ten times in a decade if you sell it after a quick 50 percent gain. If you buy businesses that will continue to increase in intrinsic value over time, the time to sell them is probably never.

Even with great risk management, forever investors will occasionally make mistakes in analysis or judgment. Moreover, the fundamentals of a business or industry may change drastically over time. Management will also change. While a forever investor has a target holding period of forever, sometimes there are reasons to sell..

Here are six reasons to sell a publicly traded business:

1. Management's integrity has become questionable.
2. You realize you made a mistake in analysis before purchasing it.

3. Competition or industry conditions have changed over time and the long-term prospects are not favorable.
4. Management personnel or its strategy has changed and you believe it is for the worse.
5. The price being offered is *substantially* above your most optimistic estimate of intrinsic value.
6. There is a far superior opportunity to reinvest the money, even after paying the capital gains tax.

Here are reasons to sell a privately owned business. If you control management, the quality of management is not a reason to sell because it can be replaced:

1. You realize you made a mistake in analysis before purchasing it.
2. Competition or industry conditions for the company have changed over time and the long-term prospects are not favorable.

It is important to acknowledge that not all businesses are great enough to be held forever. Also, a business that was once great can become poor through mismanagement, competition, and industry evolution. There are countless examples of forever investors who lost a lot of money because they didn't sell when business conditions started to deteriorate. For example, anyone who held onto shares of Chrysler, GM, Lehman Brothers, Bear Stearns, Circuit City, A&P, Borders, or Blockbuster eventually regretted not selling. Forever investors buy with the intention of holding forever, but should sell if they believe the business is going to decline in intrinsic value over time.

Developing an "Edge"

One of the first questions prospective clients will ask a money manager is "what edge do you have over other investors with the same strategy?" For example, there are literally thousands of investors who call themselves value investors. If you are a value investor, why should people put their money with you and not with one of the many other value investors?

Having a strategy that has been successful for some investors doesn't mean that you will be able to execute the strategy just as effectively. What do you do to improve the odds you are among the best at executing the strategy?

With a plethora of people flooding into investment management over the last few decades it is difficult for the typical money manager to stand out. There are plenty of smart money managers with MBAs from top universities, decades of experience, and teams of analysts. There are more smart investors in the United States than ever before, and as the population of the United States continues to grow, the number of talented investors will grow.

There is a long list of ways to improve your odds of successful execution and you should consider each one:

- Partner with someone extremely talented
- Strengthen and expand your circle of competence
- Become an expert on the history of markets and how they work
- Perform quality research and financial analysis
- Keep fees and taxes low
- Be aware of corporate change in businesses you own or desire to own
- Improve your psychological weaknesses
- Exchange ideas with like-minded investors
- Build a strong reputation so you are approached with unique investment opportunities

Notes

1. http://news.yale.edu/2015/09/24/investment-return-115-brings-yale-endowm12ent-value-256-billion.
2. Philip A. Fisher, *Common Stocks and Uncommon Profits* (New York: John Wiley & Sons, 1996), 118.
3. http://covestreetcapital.com/wp-content/uploads/2015/03/Druckenmiller-_Speech.pdf.

Chapter Six

Six Types of Common Stock Investments

There are six main types of common stock investments, as described by Peter Lynch in his investment classic *One Up on Wall Street*. The first step when researching a potential investment is to define which of the six types the company belongs and if it is suitable to your investment strategy.

In this chapter, we will discuss the six types and how they should be viewed from the forever investing perspective.

Cyclical Businesses

Highly cyclical companies often dominate the financial media's headlines because the booms and busts are fascinating. Another reason, perhaps, is because many of the very large and well-known companies are highly cyclical: airlines, autos, energy, steel, construction, raw materials, seaborne shipping, and furniture are just a few examples.

Also, many of the greatest fortunes in history were created in cyclical businesses, including the wealth of Andrew Carnegie, John D. Rockefeller, and Cornelius Vanderbilt. However, while these businesses were cyclical, the industries were in their infancy and the long-term growth potential was spectacular. Investing into a highly cyclical industry that is mature is much less enticing.

Cyclicals appeal the most to momentum investors and value investors because if they get the timing right these stocks can provide tremendous short-term returns; however, highly cyclical companies are akin to a casino in that if you stay in them long enough you might lose all your prior profits. For this reason the forever investor generally avoids highly cyclical companies, unless he or she has control of the company and can somehow mitigate risk.

Another characteristic of highly cyclical companies is the inability of management, analysts, and investors to make forecasts within a reasonable range. In 2014, when oil was $100 a barrel, oil companies and the brightest people in the industry were not predicting a crash to $30. Then when oil reached $30 no one was able to tell if it would go lower, stay at $30, or go higher over the next few years. The changes in highly cyclical companies can be quick, severe, and costly, which makes the timing of your purchase especially important.

Unlike most stocks, cyclicals are often expensive when the P/E is low, and cheap when the P/E is high. The reason for this paradox is that when a cyclical is earning historically high net income and revenue, it is often not sustainable and investors aren't willing to pay more than seven to ten times earnings. When a cyclical has peak earnings, the P/E appears cheap relative to recent growth...until earnings drop. Conversely, when a cyclical has a high P/E, it is usually in a trough and earnings are depressed.

Analysis of the balance sheet is more important for cyclicals than for companies with predictable cash flow. Cyclicals are often loaded with debt due to high capital expenditures and dividend payouts. When the industry inevitably experiences challenging times, capital to fund future capital expenditures and refinance maturing debt is difficult to raise. Moreover, interest expense can become very high and push a company into default if industry conditions become too severe and persistent.

Even in the best of times highly cyclical companies typically have capital expenditures near the cash generated from operations, resulting in no free cash flow. It is fascinating that so many of these companies with no free-cash-flow pay dividends, which results in the accumulation of debt. These companies are essentially borrowing money to pay dividends in an effort to keep the stock price high; however, when severe challenges inevitably develop the dividend is cut and the only thing left for shareholders is a steep drop in the price of the business and a huge debt burden. *Beware of companies that borrow money to support their dividends.* John D. Rockefeller Sr. advised, "Study diligently your capital requirements, and fortify yourself fully to cover possible set-backs, because you can absolutely count on set-backs."[1]

Many cyclical businesses can avoid catastrophe during the extreme booms and busts of the industry if they diversify; however, Wall Street and investors moan about companies that are not "pure plays" in an industry. If a cyclical steel company owns an industrial company that is fairly resistant to cycles, investors don't applaud the fact this makes the steel company less risky; instead they push management to break the company up and "unlock" the value of the stronger business. Private companies such as Koch Industries have a managerial advantage in that they can own a diversified group of highly cyclical and noncyclical businesses and not feel the same pressure from shareholders and Wall Street.

Stalwarts

Stalwarts are the primary target of a forever investor. These are typically midcap companies with strong competitive advantages and consistently grow organic revenue and earnings at a healthy rate.

Large-caps are usually too large to maintain high rates of organic growth and small-caps often lack strong competitive advantages. Therefore, in the midcap range is where the stalwarts tend to exist.

Due to their predictability, competitive advantages, and strong growth, stalwarts usually are defensive in market downturns, but also perform well in a rising market as a result of growing intrinsic value. Herein lies the difficultly with finding stalwarts at attractive prices: investors love them.

Another characteristic of stalwarts is that they often have a talent for strategic acquisitions to maintain a healthy growth rate and not become a slow grower. A stalwart business combined with management that is talented at capital allocation is the most any investor can ever ask.

Fast Growers

Fast growers are typically young companies that trade at high multiples based on great expectations about the company's future. Those expectations are often wildly optimistic, but on occasion some companies exceed the predicted growth. The challenge is determining when a fast grower is overvalued or undervalued.

Fast growers are tough to value because of the difficulty of predicting the growth rates. The difference between 15 percent and 20 percent compounded annual growth rates over a decade is substantial. With a 15 percent, rate earnings would increase by a total of 305 percent and with a 20 percent, rate earnings would increase over 520 percent. High expectations are often built into the current price of the stock, which makes the stock very risky if growth projections are not met.

All fast growers eventually turn into stalwarts or slow growers. This change can cause a "lost decade" when the initially high P/E causes the stock to remain flat for a decade as growth slows and the P/E gradually falls. For example, Microsoft's stock price from 1998 to 2013 returned near 0 percent despite tripling Earnings Per Share.

Slow Growers

Slow growers are companies whose organic revenue and earnings growth are in the low single digits. These companies often use free cash flow for dividends and share buybacks because the reinvestment of cash flow back into operations doesn't yield attractive returns.

Acquisitions are important to fuel growth for a slow grower and therefore the quality of management should be given careful attention. Management eager to show growth may overpay for an acquisition and destroy shareholder value, while patient and astute management will make acquisitions that add substantial shareholder value. Slow growers can increase intrinsic value at rates similar to stalwarts if management is exceptional at capital allocation. Platform companies are often industry consolidators of slow growing niche businesses.

Turnarounds

Turnarounds are companies with serious challenges to their operations, not companies in a temporary down cycle. Turnarounds frequently look enticing to bargain hunters based on book value or P/E, but they sell at low multiples because they have serious challenges.

Unless you plan to take over management and turn around the company yourself, the best time to buy a turnaround is when there is evidence of a turnaround already in place. You won't get in at the bottom, but you have eliminated a lot of risk and uncertainty.

You should also avoid a turnaround situation unless it is right in the center of your circle of competence, not around the edges. Warren Buffett made an investment into GEICO when it was in trouble because he had invested into the company years earlier and knew the business very well. Buffett knew that if GEICO could strengthen its balance sheet and survive the short-term losses, it could write better policies going forward and fully recover. Similarly, Ted Weschler made his investment into the bankrupt W. R. Grace because he understood it as well as anyone after working for the company early in his career.

Investors in turnarounds must keep a close eye on the company bonds, balance sheet, and cash flow. When a company's bonds are trading at 20 cents on the dollar, the bond market is telling us the company is in serious trouble. If that company turns around, those bonds will rise five-fold from 20 cents to a dollar. If the company defaults on bond payments, common stock holders will likely get wiped out. There is no reason to own the common stock of a company whose bonds are trading at prices that indicate a default may occur in the near future. If you are confident the company will turn around, the distressed debt is likely a less risky option.

Asset Plays

Asset plays are investments based on break-up value or sum-of-the-parts. They may include hidden assets that are underreported on the balance sheet, such as real estate, or assets that are marked-to-market but expected to substantially rise in value.

Asset plays usually require an activist shareholder to pressure management to unlock the value of the underappreciated asset because management will be resistant to selling assets. A common and major mistake many investors make is that they don't give enough weight to the risk that asset values might decrease. Even if the asset maintains its value, it may take years to sell assets and there will be heavy legal expenses and taxes. These are important considerations.

Edward Lampert's purchase of Kmart is an interesting case study in asset plays. He is a brilliant investor, became a billionaire at forty-two years old, and was frequently called a genius by other accomplished investment professionals.

Kmart filed for bankruptcy in 2002 and Lampert purchased its bonds in an effort to take control of the company. He brought Kmart out of bankruptcy in 2003 and merged it with Sears in 2004, forming the Sears Holding Company. After emerging from bankruptcy in 2003, the stock went from $15 to a peak of $180 in 2007.

Lampert was attracted to Kmart for its vast real-estate portfolio. The retail business of Kmart was not going well, but as long as it was operating at break even or better, Lampert likely figured it was a huge bargain because of the real estate that could be sold.

It is true that the real estate was worth many times the price of the company when Lampert acquired it, but he underestimated how long it would take him to unload that real estate and how unprofitable the stores would become.

After years of spinning off assets such as Land's End, Sears Canada, and real estate, Sears Holding is now trading near $15 again. The first few years it appeared to be a brilliant investment, but it has turned into a poor investment because of the illiquidity of his position. Many investors who admire Edward Lampert, myself included, road his coattails and invested alongside him in 2003, but sold out above $100 when the company was at a high valuation and the retailer was showing signs of declining sales and profits. Having control over a company can be a disadvantage when operations are struggling and you want to sell.

The Evolution of a Company

Companies change from one investment type to another over time. For example, Apple can be categorized as different investment types during different times in its history. When Apple was founded it was a venture capital investment and highly speculative. Once it started to produce computers and generate sales, it became a growth company. Then, around the time Steve Jobs resigned, it was a struggling slow grower.

When Steve Jobs came back to Apple in the late 1990s, the company was in trouble (i.e., a turnaround). Then, as Apple redesigned the Mac computer and invented iTunes and the iPod, it became a growth stock.

Today Apple is the largest company in the world by market cap and is no longer a growth company. It is difficult to categorize Apple as a stalwart because it operates in fast-changing industries that are unpredictable; Apple is most likely a slow grower.

Apple used to be a favorite of growth investors, and value investors scoffed at the high multiples, but today it gets a lot of attention from bargain hunters—paradoxically at a much higher price than when they thought it was overvalued—because it trades at ten times earnings.

As an investor it is important to understand the six investment types, how each type behaves, and the evolution of a company.

Notes
1. John D. Rockefeller Sr, *Random Reminiscences of Men and Events* (Creative English Publishing, 2013), 96.

Chapter Seven

Investor Psychology

Most people have the brain power and experience to be successful investors, but few have the required psychological makeup. The greatest investors are cerebral, while the worst are often the ones calling his or her advisor every two weeks to discuss the portfolio movements. Emotional investors are better off avoiding publicly traded stocks entirely and investing into bonds, real estate, and privately owned businesses.

There is no shame in avoiding publicly traded stocks if your temperament is not suited to the wild swings. Andrew Carnegie is undoubtedly one of the greatest investors in US history, yet even he avoided publicly traded stocks. In his autobiography, Carnegie wrote about the psychological challenges of investing into publicly traded businesses. It also has implications for Boards and CEOs that focus too much on the company's stock price and not its underlying value:

> I have never bought or sold a share of stock speculatively in my life, except one small lot of Pennsylvania Railroad shares that I bought early in life for investment and for which I did not pay at the time because bankers offered to carry it for me at a low rate. I have adhered to the rule never to purchase what I did not pay for, and never to sell what I did not own. In those early days, however, I had several interests that were taken over in the course of business. They included some stocks and securities that were quoted on the New York Stock Exchange, and I found that when I opened my paper in the morning I was tempted to look first at the quotations of the stock market. As I had determined to sell all my interests in every outside concern and concentrate my attention upon our manufacturing concerns in Pittsburgh, I further resolved not even to own any stock that was bought and sold upon any stock exchange. With the exception of trifling amounts which came to me in various ways I have adhered strictly to this rule.
>
> Such a course should commend itself to every man in the manufacturing business and to all professional men. For

the manufacturing man especially the rule would seem all-important. His mind must be kept calm and free if he is to decide wisely the problems which are continually coming before him. Nothing tells in the long run like good judgment, and no sound judgment can remain with the man whose mind is disturbed by the mercurial changes of the Stock Exchange. It places him under an influence akin to intoxication. What is not, he sees, and what he sees, is not. He cannot judge of relative values or get the true perspective of things. The molehill seems to him a mountain and the mountain a molehill, and he jumps at conclusions which he should arrive at by reason. His mind is upon the stock quotations and not upon the points that require calm thought.[1]

If you do buy publicly traded stocks, there are important psychological advantages of investing into outstanding businesses with the intention of owning them forever. When you own a weak company and the stock price falls, you probably don't want to own more because you'll be overexposed to a poor business. However, when you own a great company and the price falls, you'll probably want to buy more shares since the price is cheaper.

Another psychological advantage is that if there are tough economic times and the economy is not doing well, it is stressful if you own a portfolio of weak businesses that get hit hard. If you own a portfolio of outstanding businesses you can be confident the current challenges are temporary because the businesses will increase sales and free cash flow over time. Owners of outstanding businesses sleep better at night.

Investor Psychology Is More Important than IQ

A low IQ will likely prevent someone from becoming a talented investor, but a high IQ does not ensure investment success. Someone with an IQ of 160 won't necessarily be a better investor than someone with an IQ of 120.

Two popular examples of high IQ people getting poor investment results are Isaac Newton and Long-Term Capital Management.

Sir Isaac Newton was undoubtedly one of the most brilliant people to ever live. His many and substantial contributions to mathematics and physics are astounding. Yet, even Isaac Newton let emotion get the best of him when it came to investing.

In 1720, Isaac Newton owned shares in the South Sea Company, a "hot" stock in England at the time. Newton earned a quick 100 percent gain of 7,000 pounds. However, shares of the South Sea Company kept rising, and Newton bought back in at a higher price and lost 20,000 pounds—equivalent to roughly $3 million today.[2]

Sir Isaac Newton was a genius, but when it came to investing he was as ordinary as any amateur investor that succumbs to emotional whims. He was lured in by the euphoric prospect of "quick money" and in his analysis didn't put enough emphasis on how he was exposing himself to substantial risk.

The story of Long-Term Capital Management (LTCM), as chronicled by Roger Lowenstein in his book *When Genius Failed*, is also a testament to why high IQ is not a guarantee of high returns. LTCM was a hedge fund formed with arguably the best resume of any fund ever to exist. It was founded by one of the best bond traders on Wall Street, employed two Nobel-prize winning economists, and five partners had PhDs from MIT with backgrounds in arbitrage or working for the Federal Reserve.

In its first few years the fund was the envy of Wall Street. A $1 million investment when the fund opened in March 1994 was worth $4 million by March 1998.[3]

The fund engaged in arbitrage transactions, which means it looked for price discrepancies among similar securities trading in different markets. These trades provided very small gains that were "sure things" and the fund would use enormous amounts of cheap leverage to maximize profits. The fund also made large bets on swaps and equity volatility.

In mid-1998 some trades started going the wrong way and because the fund was so leveraged it was impossible to wait for them to recover. In September 1998, the fund collapsed and investors ended up losing more than 90 percent of their money.

The positions were so large and illiquid that the Federal Reserve had to bail out the hedge fund. The partners at one point had $1.9 billion of their own money in the fund, which was nearly completely wiped out.[4]

The legal troubles of a former congressman is an example outside of investing that demonstrates the difference between a high IQ and wise decision-making. He was a Rhodes Scholar with a master's in public administration from Harvard before being elected into office. A few years into his political career he was arrested for having sexual relations with an underage campaign volunteer. While serving his sentence, he was also convicted of bank fraud and misusing campaign funds for personal use. In 2015 he was convicted of failure to file tax returns for 2009 through 2012, and then missed his arraignment.

When it comes to investing, as with most vocations, IQ matters only to a certain point. A person with an IQ of 120 who has the right temperament, values, and character will get much further than the person with a 160 IQ who has the wrong temperament, values, and character.

Peter Thiel's Theory of Determinism and Optimism

Peter Thiel is a cofounder of PayPal and early investor in Facebook. He is also one of the most respected thinkers in Silicon Valley. Thiel says there are four types of attitudes towards the future and I've elaborated to show that each requires a different investment strategy.

- The *definite optimist* has a concrete plan for the future and strongly believes in that future being better than today. This is someone who is likely to be an entrepreneur or have a concentrated portfolio of investments.
- The *indefinite optimist* is bullish on the future but lacks any design and plan for how to make such a future possible. This is someone who is likely to invest using Modern Portfolio Theory and broad diversification.

- The *definite pessimist* has a specific vision for the future but believes that future to be bleak. This is someone who likely shorts stocks and owns bonds.
- The *indefinite pessimist* has a bearish view on the future but no idea what to do about it. This is likely someone who has most of their investable assets in cash and US Treasuries.

Pay Attention to the Crowds, but Dissent When Appropriate

Hetty Green was a shrewd and powerful investor in the early 1900s. She inherited a fortune, lived frugally, and grew her net worth through investing. There have been very few people in American history who inherited a large sum of money and went on to grow it more than fifteen-fold merely through investing. That vast majority of the people who inherit fortunes are much better at spending than investing.

In 1865, at the age of thirty, Hetty inherited $5.7 million and another $600,000 within the next decade. At the time of her death in 1916, she was reportedly worth $100 million.[5] While the compounded annual return comes out to roughly 6 percent on her inheritance, she had large cash reserves, spent money on living expenses, and bailed her husband out of $702,000 in debt when she was fifty years old.[6] Her actual return on investment was likely a few percent better and she is a perfect example that the key to a lifetime of investment success is not to make brilliant and complex investments, but to avoid doing foolish things.

In November 1905, Hetty told a *New York Times* reporter: "I buy when things are low and no one wants them. I keep them…until they go up and people are anxious to buy. That is the general secret of business success."[7]

In other words, Hetty was a value investor, or bargain hunter, long before Benjamin Graham and David Dodd wrote *Security Analysis*. She was also a contrarian long before David Dreman wrote books on the merits of going against the crowds.

While going against the crowd sometimes is necessary for investment success, it is psychologically difficult to disagree with other smart people. Most people interpret your disagreement with their opinions as an insult or condemnation. Sticking to an unpopular position that requires time to develop when clients and shareholders are questioning you is the toughest test money-managers encounter. Being wrong when others agree with you hurts your bank account, but being wrong when others disagree with you hurts both your bank account and reputation. In other words, investors going against the crowd must place extra emphasis on keeping mistakes small.

Focus, Discipline, and Awareness

At a dinner hosted by Bill Gates's father, Warren Buffett said the most important thing in getting to where he'd gotten in life was "focus." And Bill Gates said the same thing.[8] Buffett didn't elaborate on what he meant by "focus." He might have meant his ability to focus on specific goals and not spreading his attention to various endeavors. He might have meant being disciplined by sticking within his circle of competence or to his investment approach when it has been criticized. Regardless of which meaning he intended, both definitions of "focus" are important.

Great awareness is also of paramount significance. Notice when you are forcing yourself to look at companies that test the boundaries of your circle of competence because there is nothing more attractive to buy. Also notice when you are considering a purchase of a company you might not want to own forever. One of the hardest things in investing, especially when managing money, is to do nothing. However, there are times when it is the wisest thing to do.

Great investors are disciplined, but they are not inflexible. If a rare opportunities arises which is certain to provide outstanding returns with minimal risk, it makes sense to take advantage of the opportunity, even if it causes a deviation from your strategy. An investor might find a few of these opportunities in his or her lifetime. In other words, be disciplined and focused on your investment strategy, but not inflexible if a rare outstanding opportunity is presented to you and is outside of your strategy.

Overcoming Setbacks and Mistakes

I have known men, personally, who have met with pecuniary
reverses, and absolutely committed suicide, because they thought
they could never overcome their misfortune. But I have known
others who have met more serious financial difficulties, and have
bridged them over by simple perseverance, aided by a firm belief
they were doing justly, and that Providence would "overcome
evil with good."

—P. T. Barnum[9]

Never give in, never give in, never, never, never—in nothing,
great or small, large or petty.

—Winston Churchill

Avoiding mistakes and failure should be the first goal of any
investor; however, people are not infallible and mistakes happen.
The difference between success and failure is often how we
respond to adversity. When you inevitably suffer setbacks, faith
and fortitude will help you overcome those obstacles.

There is a tale about identical twin brothers who grew up
with an alcoholic father. One of the twins became an alcoholic
and the other never drank alcohol. Interviewers asked the one
twin why he thought he was an alcoholic and he responded,
"Growing up with an alcoholic father, it had an impact on me."
The interviewers posed the same question to the other brother,
asking him why he thought he never drank alcohol, and he
responded, "Growing up with an alcoholic father, it had an
impact on me." The moral of the tale is that what happens to you
shapes your character, but what it shapes it into is determined by
how you respond.

Faith and fortitude are character traits of successful people in
nearly every field, including investing. Two examples of
investors who overcame mistakes and went on to become
multibillionaires are Bill Ackman and Carl Icahn.

Bill Ackman deserves tremendous respect for his
extraordinary reemergence as a hedge-fund manager; it is

unprecedented. He cofounded Gotham Partners in 1992, fresh out of Harvard Business School. Due to illiquid investments in golf courses that were loaded with debt, Ackman had to wind down his fund in 2002. In 2004 he opened a new fund, Pershing Square, with $4 million of his own money and $50 million from the company Leucadia. Despite some high-profile mistakes in Borders, J. C. Penney, and Valeant, Pershing Square has done exceptionally well, and by the end of 2014 reached a peak of over $18 billion in assets under management.

Ackman's positions in companies earn him as much media attention as Warren Buffett and Carl Icahn, and much of it is not flattering. Being a public figure opens you up to a great deal of rancor and vitriolic behavior. Furthermore, a hedge-fund manager is one of the most controversial professions among a certain part of our population.

Ackman is one of the most successful and heavily criticized money managers, with skin is as thick as that of a politician. If Ackman has a motto it is probably of the saying, "There is only one way to avoid criticism: do nothing, say nothing, and be nothing."

Carl Icahn has had one of the most fascinating careers in investing. When he was twenty-six years old he was already making great money. He bought a convertible and had a model girlfriend; however, he was highly leveraged and in 1962 there was a crash that wiped him out in one day. He said he doesn't remember which disappeared quicker, the model or the car.

Many people have lost confidence and left Wall Street after losing big, but Carl Icahn knew that he was not done—he just had to start over. He thought it best to develop a niche, so Icahn became one of the leading experts on options. He built a large commission base and bought a seat on the NYSE in 1968. He also engaged in arbitrage on convertible securities.

In the 1980s he became famous in the business world for his activist positions in companies (dubbed "corporate raider" back then). Instead of focusing on companies with great management, Icahn sought good companies that could use better management, and then replaced the management. Sometimes he would even split up a company, which caused an uproar from those it negatively impacted. Being a high-profile activist investor will certainly not win you any popularity contests; however, investors should thank Icahn because he has been one of the most influential shareholder rights' activists of the last few decades.

While Icahn is an activist investor, he is not inflexible in his approach. He has also taken non-activist positions in companies with strong management, such as Apple and Netflix. Icahn knows there is more than one way to make money by investing into businesses and he is darn good at making money.

There are some investments that Icahn held for only a few years, but he has also owned some businesses for three decades. At the end of 2015 his net worth was estimated to be $20 billion, earning him a reputation as one of the greatest investors of all time.

Even if you have the brains, not everyone has the thick skin to do what Ackman and Icahn have done. Nobody wants to be disliked or routinely criticized. It is especially painful when your children hear people calling you names. It would get tiresome for anyone, and Ackman and Icahn seem to have worked on their public relations in recent years.

No matter how talented you are, if you spend a lifetime in business and investing, you will have periods of severe losses, lawsuits, and other causes of stress. In fact, if lawyers are not trying to get settlements from you or your business, you probably aren't that successful yet.

Warren Buffett has one of the most enviable long-term track records, but even he has had setbacks. Berkshire Hathaway has declined 50 percent on three different occasions since Buffett bought it fifty years ago. Also, a company controlled by Buffett and Munger, Blue Chip Stamps, was investigated by the SEC in the 1970s for bidding up securities on a company. Blue Chip was fined by the SEC, but it could have gone worse. Buffett also suffered great stress with a Salomon Brothers investment in the 1990s. Shortly after he made an investment in Salomon there was a scandal because a trader made false bids for Treasury bonds, putting the entire company on the brink of collapse; Buffett had to step in as temporary CEO.

In his book, *Good Profit*, Charles Koch said despite its long-term success, Koch Industries has suffered several setbacks, including oil spills in the 1990s; however, once the adversity is over, it makes you more prepared for the future.[10]

Billionaire hedge-fund manager David Einhorn tells the story in his book, *Fooling Some of the People All of the Time,* about how fickle clients can be if you are a money manager. One of his largest clients was a semiretired and well-known hedge-fund manager. After five bad months in 1998, the client called Einhorn's team to his office and said "I thought you were moneymakers!" The client withdrew his funds as soon as possible and for the next five years Einhorn would on occasion hear from someone who met the former client and was told Einhorn was lousy. Over a six-month period in 1998–1999, about half the clients withdrew from the fund.[11] Imagine losing half your clients because of a bad few months.

No matter how hard you try to avoid stress, there will occasionally be tough challenges; it is part of business and investing. However, not everyone handles stress and anxiety in the same way. Chronic and severe stress can cause a normally optimistic person to become depressed or develop an anxiety disorder.

For example, Bernie Madoff's son committed suicide after struggling to cope with the humiliation of what his father had done. Two days before Christmas in 2008, the former CFO of Lehman Brothers was hospitalized for attempting suicide by overdosing on sleeping pills. In 2009, a German billionaire committed suicide after debt became a huge burden at his companies and he feared losing control of his businesses. Also in 2009, the CFO of Freddie Mac committed suicide from mounting stress during the Financial Crisis. These were well-off, highly educated people who lost the will to live due to chronic stress.

A favorite poem of mine is *Richard Cory* by Edwin Arlington Robinson. It is a reminder that people can appear to have it all, but you don't know what is going on with them internally.

Whenever Richard Cory went down town,
We people on the pavement looked at him:
He was a gentleman from sole to crown,
Clean favored, and imperially slim.

And he was always quietly arrayed,
And he was always human when he talked;
But still he fluttered pulses when he said,
"Good-morning," and he glittered when he walked.

And he was rich—yes, richer than a king—
And admirably schooled in every grace:
In fine, we thought that he was everything
To make us wish that we were in his place.

So on we worked, and waited for the light,
And went without the meat, and cursed the bread;
And Richard Cory, one calm summer night,
Went home and put a bullet through his head.

We tend to think that people who suffer from anxiety disorders or depression are mentally weak. But was Abraham Lincoln weak?

Abraham Lincoln is a model of perseverance. His numerous failings in business and politics have been recorded. What has not been given considerable attention, until the book *Lincoln's Melancholy* shined a spotlight on the subject, is that Lincoln likely suffered from "clinical depression." In 1835 and in 1841, it is documented that Lincoln suffered severe "episodes" of depression and was suicidal. He was so suicidal; in fact, that he refused to carry a pocketknife out of fear of what he might do with it.[12]

If you are an investor or entrepreneur who struggles coping with stress, you should give serious consideration to taking on a partner. A partner will not only help you with risk management, but he or she can be a voice of calm during stressful periods.

There is also comfort in knowing you are not alone. Nearly all the investors profiled in this book have taken on partners or hired managers who play the roles of a partner.

Two brains are likely to be more emotionally intelligent than one.

It Is Easier to Be Resilient When Young

Major business setbacks are more difficult to deal with once you are older and have a family. Many of the great stories about entrepreneurs who failed and went on to create exceptional businesses were young when they failed. A business failing or major setback in your fifties or sixties gives you less time to start over again. Moreover, achieving success and then losing everything has a far greater emotional impact than failing before ever having achieved success.

Henry J. Heinz founded a business in 1869, at the age of twenty-five, to sell bottled horseradish. The business failed in 1875 and Heinz was forced to declare bankruptcy. Heinz couldn't start another company until his debt was paid off, so the next year he joined his cousin and brother at their company, which had recently added ketchup to the product line. In 1888, Heinz took control of the company and renamed it H. J. Heinz Company.

When Walt Disney was eighteen he founded his first company, Iwerks-Disney Commercial Artists, but it wasn't bringing in money, so Disney and his partner took jobs elsewhere. At the age of twenty he founded another company in Kansas City, called Laugh-O-Gram. Twice his business had to move offices in the middle of the night because it couldn't pay the rent. Disney for a time also slept on rolls of canvas and cushions in the office to save money.[13] The business never took off, and at the age of twenty-one Disney declared bankruptcy and moved to Hollywood to start over.

Milton Hershey also had early setbacks. He opened a candy store in Philadelphia, but it failed within a few years. He moved to New York to open another candy store, but it also failed. Then, at the age of twenty-six and twice failed in business, he started the Lancaster Caramel Company, which sold caramel candy in bulk. By chance a man from England came through town, liked the caramels, and placed large orders that helped fuel the company's growth. Hershey sold the Lancaster Caramel Company after fourteen years and used the proceeds to start the Hershey Chocolate Company.

Henry Ford founded his first company, the Detroit Automobile Company, at the age of thirty-six, but the company went under within two years. In the same year as the Detroit Automobile Company closed, Ford opened a new company, the Henry Ford Company. However, within a year he left the company and it was renamed the Cadillac Automobile Company. After two failed attempts at starting an automobile company, at the age of thirty-nine he started the company that would later be renamed the Ford Motor Company.

In 1953, Charlie Munger was twenty-nine years old when he and his wife of eight years got divorced. Munger lost the little he had in the divorce and his wife kept the family home. Shortly after the split, he learned that his son had leukemia. Munger would go into the hospital, hold his young son, and then walk the streets crying. One year after the diagnosis, his son died.

Munger was thirty-one years old, divorced, broke, and burying his nine-year-old son. As devastating as these events were, Charlie Munger overcame the suffering and became a multibillionaire, as well as one of the most respected business thinkers of the past few decades.

While recovering from failure is never easy, it is easier when you are young and haven't lost much. However, it is still possible to overcome setbacks at an older age. No matter your age, tenacity and resilience are essential for business and investment success. There will be challenging times, and how you react to those challenges may be the difference between winning and losing.

Notes

1. Andrew Carnegie, *The Autobiography of Andrew Carnegie and the Gospel of Wealth* (New York: New American Library, a division of Penguin Group, 2006), 136.
2. Benjamin Graham with commentary by Jason Zweig. *The Intelligent Investor.* Revised Edition 2006. First Collins Business Essentials. Page 13.
3. Roger Lowenstein, *When Genius Failed: The Rise and Fall of Long-Term Capital Management* (New York: Random House Trade Paperback Edition, 2001), xvi.
4. Ibid., 219.
5. Charles Slack, *Hetty: The Genius and Madness of America's First Female Tycoon* (New York: Ecco, an imprint of HarperCollins, 2004), ix.
6. Ibid., 97.
7. Ibid., 166.
8. Alice Schroeder, *The Snowball: Warren Buffett and the Business of Life* (New York: Bantam Books, a Division of Random House, 2008), 623.
9. P.T. Barnum. *The Art of Getting Money* (Seaside, OR: Watchmaker Publishing, 2010), 30.
10. Charles G. Koch, *Good Profit: How Creating Value for Others Built One of the World's Most Successful Companies* (New York: Penguin Random House, 2015), 81.
11. David Einhorn, *Fooling Some of the People All of the Time: A Long Short Story* (Hoboken, NJ: John Wiley & Sons, Inc., 2008), 32.
12. Joshua Wolf Shenk. *Lincoln's Melancholy: How Depression Challenged a President and Fueled His Greatness* (New York: First Mariner Books, 2006), 38–39.
13. Neal Gabler, *Walt Disney: The Triumph of the American Imagination* (New York: Alfred A. Knopf a division of Random House, 2006), 71.

Chapter Eight

Destroyers of Wealth: Inflation and Taxes

Investors have three top priorities. The first priority is not to lose money. The second priority is to beat inflation, after taxes. The third is to earn strong returns for his or her strategy, after taxes.

In other words, inflation and taxes deserve careful consideration with regards to one's investment approach.

Inflation in the United States

The Consumer Price Index (CPI) is designed to be a measure of the inflation rate for the average person in the United States, but keep in mind that your inflation rate might be different than the Bureau of Labor Statistics estimate. For example, if housing is 60 percent of your spending or 20 percent of your spending, your inflation rate is different than the CPI rate, which weights housing at 42 percent. If you spend, or need to spend in the future, more or less than 8 percent on medical care or 7 percent on education, then your inflation rate is different than the CPI.

As an investor you cannot do anything about inflation, but it is imperative to comprehend the causes and effects of it.

As the saying goes, those who understand compound interest, earn it; those who don't understand it, pay it. And inflation is a compounding expense that we all must pay.

Inflation is a cruel destroyer of wealth because the annual changes in prices are often so subtle that we ignore the implications. Aside from economists, few people pay attention to inflation. The average person's lifestyle isn't changed if the Consumer Price Index is up 2 percent to 3 percent this year, therefore they don't reflect much on the long-term repercussions.

While the annual inflation rate is so small that it is often ignored, the compounded effects over longer periods of time have a substantial impact on your purchasing power. If inflation averages 3 percent over a twenty-five-year period, your purchasing power will be cut in half. In other words, you have to earn 3 percent after-tax just to maintain your level of wealth. If you are in a high-tax bracket, you will have to earn 4 percent to 5 percent before-tax to maintain your current level of wealth.

Since the Great Depression, the annual inflation rate in the United States has reached as high as 14.4 percent in 1947 and 13.5 percent in 1980. There is no guarantee that inflation will not reach double-digits again in your lifetime, and that must be incorporated into your investment strategy. Investing all of your money today into thirty-year US Treasuries yielding 3 percent is an extremely risky thing to do with your money for the next thirty years. At best you are likely to break even after inflation.

Taxes

Taxes have played an important economic role throughout the history of the United States—especially during war times—but they have also played an important political role.

After the Seven Years' War with the French, England was in need of tax revenue. British taxes per capita were among the highest in the world, while the American colonies were among the lowest. The British felt that the colonies were getting national defense from England at a low cost and proposed two acts to raise taxes on the colonies: the Sugar Act of 1764 and Stamp Act of 1765.

The colonists believed the Sugar Act contained provisions that helped British businesses at the expense of colonial businesses. The Stamp Act also incited political tempers to a boil, which was the first step toward rebellion. Americans were so outraged they began boycotting English goods.

Parliament responded to the economic pressure by repealing the Stamp Act, but maintained it had the right to tax the colonies. In 1767, new Prime Minister Charles Townshend imposed duties on such items as tea, glass, paper, and red and white lead. Americans became outraged not only at the duties but also at the steps England took to strictly enforce them. Resistance spread and protests were held, leading to the Boston Massacre in 1770, which left five colonials dead. Americans again boycotted British imports and English merchants exerted pressure to change the trade policy. All the duties were repealed, except the duty on tea.[1]

The Tea Act of 1773 brought about new resistance. The new act allowed the East India Company to ship tea directly to the colonies, avoiding double taxation from shipping it to Britain and then again to America. The intention was to sell more tea at a lower price, which upset smugglers in America. The American smugglers were undersold by the East India Company, importers were removed from the picture, and colonials were paying taxes on the tea. Merchants and shopkeepers had a swift and violent reaction. Tea was sent back to England or destroyed—the most spectacular of which was the Boston Tea Party.[2]

The possibilities for peaceful reconciliation quickly passed. Violence broke out with the shots of April 19, 1775, which marked a major turning point in the history of the world. On July 4, 1776, independence was declared.[3]

Many people, even ones with college educations, fail to realize that federal income taxes in the United States were virtually nonexistent from 1776 to 1913. In 1894, Congress passed income-tax legislation, but the Supreme Court declared it unconstitutional. Congress then appealed to the American people by saying the country needs an income tax to fund an expansion of our military and it would be more efficient than tariffs. In 1909, Congress passed the Sixteenth Amendment to the Constitution, which allowed a federal income tax—it was ratified in 1913.[4] Once the federal government was granted the power to charge income taxes, it was like a college freshman with his or her first credit card and it went on a spending spree. The government found more and more ways to take from taxpayers and spend it. New taxes included Capital Gains Tax (1913), Estate Tax (1916), Social Security Tax (1935) and Medicare Tax (1966). The highest marginal federal income tax bracket went from 7 percent in 1913, to 77 percent in 1918, to 94 percent in 1944. It stayed above 70 percent until 1981, and in 2016 is roughly 40 percent.

The highest corporate tax rate also went from 1 percent in 1915, to 40 percent in 1942, and 52 percent in 1952. However, the government had far more ideas to spend American taxpayers' hard-earned money than dollars it brought in from all these burdensome taxes, so it managed to get us $20 trillion into debt!

With the rise of big federal government, states saw little of that money. Therefore, state and local governments also require taxes to pay for education, police, fire fighters, parks, and other programs. Property tax was one method by which local governments brought in revenue since colonial times, but a rise in spending led to sales tax and an income tax in all but a few states.

Entrepreneurs and businesses are drivers of our economy. They create the products, services, jobs, and government revenue. We need talented entrepreneurs, executives, and investors who are willing to take financial and reputational risks.

There are three main reasons why the government confiscating excessive amounts of money from families and companies can harm economic progress:

(1) Entrepreneurs and businesses take big risks and often fail. They are willing to take the risks because if they succeed, they are well rewarded. An increase in taxes results in the rewards becoming lower, but the risks remain just as high. In other words, the expected returns from starting a new business are lower as taxes rise.

(2) Wealthy people are a primary source of venture capital. A family that has a net worth of $200,000 is not going to use all that $200,000 to finance a stranger in his or her new business venture; however, a person with a net worth of $20 million might find it less risky to spend 1 percent of his or her wealth to finance the business venture. The wealthy person is willing to invest because the rewards might be high. If the government takes away most of the rewards through high taxes, people will be less willing to invest into new businesses that desperately need that capital.

(3) The more the government takes from companies, the less those companies can reinvest after taxes. When a company that makes medical devices has more money to

invest into innovation, it improves our standard of living over time. When Home Depot has more money to open new stores, it creates jobs and helps people who need a Home Depot in their city. When a profitable industrial company pays less in taxes, it has more cash flow to invest into improving safety, upgrading facilities, and competing with foreign companies. It also has the ability to pay workers higher wages.

In other words, high taxes discourage entrepreneurship, innovation, and financing of businesses. However, the damage doesn't end there. If you are a hardworking middle-class family that saves and invests, your greatest expense is not research, investment advisory services, or losing money from mistakes—it is taxes.

If you earn money from your job or business, you pay federal, state, and local taxes. After paying those taxes, you have living expenses and sales tax on nearly everything you purchase. If you are lucky enough to have any money left after the high taxes and living expenses, you can invest it. However, if you invest it and make a profit, the government will tax you again!

Your goal as an investor is to make as much money as possible after-tax. Therefore, understanding how you can save on taxes is just as important as any other investment decision.

The government has nonvoting ownership rights in every profitable business in the United States, which amounts to roughly 35 percent of the *pretax* profits. If you own 35 percent of a C-corporation, you get 35 percent of the profits *after-tax*. In other words, the government has by far the largest stake of the profits in almost every corporation in the United States.

Imagine you own 50 percent of a company, and last year that company earned $100 million before-tax and paid $35 million in taxes. Of the $65 million in profit remaining after taxes, your 50 percent ownership entitles you to $32.5 million in profits. In other words, the government's stake in corporate America is greater than a 50 percent shareholder's after-tax. But that is not the full extent of the taxation. If the profits of the corporation are actually distributed to you, the government will charge another 15 percent dividend tax!

Taxes were not always this high in the United States. Proponents of "big-government" might try to find a correlation between US economic growth and tax rates and declare that high taxes don't impact US economic growth and technology growth. After all, the United States made monumental advances in healthcare, technology, and standards of living in the twentieth century despite the high tax burden.

The argument is correct that the tax burden is not currently at a level where most people and companies feel too discouraged to invest in new businesses; however, that doesn't mean that there are not important opportunity costs of high taxes. Only people who oppose freedom believe that stripping people of their money through high taxes is inherently good and letting people keep their money is bad. The people in the United States who advocate for high taxes generally believe that government spending is good, not high taxes. Taxes strip individuals of their liberty and the right to keep the money they earn.

The other concern with high taxes is that immigrants such as Elon Musk (Tesla), Jerry Yang (Yahoo), Pierre Omidyar (Ebay), and Sergey Brin (Google) will not come to the United States. Right now we attract immigrants because of our free enterprise system, high-quality universities, talented workforce, and scale as the largest economy in the world. In our current environment, the benefits for highly intelligent future entrepreneurs immigrating to the United States outweigh the high costs of doing business here, but it is something we must keep in mind.

Federal taxes are not so high as to discourage immigration or cause people to leave the United States, but there are people who move out of high-tax states to low-tax states such as Florida. Hedge-fund manager David Tepper has a net worth estimated to be over $10 billion and he has worked in New Jersey for the last two decades. New Jersey's top income tax rate is nearly 9 percent and it also has an estate tax and inheritance tax. The top 1 percent of income earners in New Jersey account for one-third of the state's revenue from personal income taxes. David Tepper's move to Florida, which has no personal state income tax and no estate taxes, has caused budget concerns in New Jersey.

Wyoming is a beautiful state with no personal income tax and no corporate income tax. The reason young entrepreneurs are not moving to Wyoming is because the costs still outweigh the tax benefits. One of the most important considerations of new businesses is clustering, with Silicon Valley being the prime example. If you are a new tech start-up, you are not likely to move to Wyoming where taxes are lowest, you are probably going to move to Silicon Valley with its high California taxes and expensive real estate because that is where you believe you'll attract the best employees, venture capitalists, and make the right connections. Hedge-fund managers open funds in Manhattan despite the huge tax burden because they believe the networking and capital raising will outweigh the high taxes. In other words, money managers move to Manhattan and tech firms move to Silicon Valley because they believe they will earn more after-tax in those places, despite the high taxes.

As an individual you are acutely aware that the more the government takes from you on an annual basis, the less you have to save and invest. The financially astute understand tax laws and use methods to legally minimize their taxes. As an investor, short-term investing is the least prudent way to invest if you are trying to minimize taxes, while forever investing is the most sensible.

The table below shows $1 invested at 15 percent annually. The table illustrates that an investor's tax rate and holding period have substantial impacts on the after-tax return. In the first column is the tax-free rate, which is for retirement accounts and nonprofit institutions. The second column is the 40 percent short-term tax, which is for investors or corporations in the highest tax bracket that don't hold investments for more than one year. The bottom column is for an investor who owns a stock and doesn't sell it until year ten.

	Y 1	Y 2	Y 3	Y 4	Y 5	Y 6	Y 7	Y 8	Y 9	Y 10
Tax-Free	$1.15	$1.32	$1.52	$1.75	$2.01	$2.31	$2.66	$3.06	$3.52	$4.05
40% Short-Term Tax	$1.09	$1.19	$1.30	$1.41	$1.54	$1.68	$1.83	$1.99	$2.17	$2.37
20% Capital Gains Tax	$1.15	$1.32	$1.52	$1.75	$2.01	$2.31	$2.66	$3.06	$3.52	$3.44

As an individual you have no say in what tax rates will be, but you cannot ignore their impact. Forever investing is the most tax-efficient way to invest.

Notes

1. Gary M. Walton and Hugh Rockoff, *History of the American Economy*, 11th ed. (Mason, OH: South-Western, Cengage Learning, 2010), 98–99.
2. Ibid., 99.
3. Ibid., 101.
4. Ibid., 374.

Chapter Nine

Purposeful Investing

A business that makes nothing but money is a poor business.

—Henry Ford

Businesses provide enormous economic and societal benefits, but entrepreneurs and business owners are not driven by altruism; they work grueling hours, undertake substantial financial risks, spend more time than most away from their families, and cope with the heavy stress because they want to make profits. Adam Smith famously said it this way: "It is not from the benevolence of the butcher, the brewer, or the baker, that we expect our dinner, but from their regard to their own interest."

Investors also contribute to economic prosperity by providing capital to entrepreneurs and businesses. Investors do not risk their capital because they not only want to help the economy but also want to make profits. The typical investor allocates his or her capital to investments which will provide the highest risk-adjusted return. There are, however, some exceptions.

A life devoted to "things" is a shallow and meaningless life; therefore, once people sustain an income or net worth above that needed to live comfortably (or luxuriously), they often try to use their money for a greater purpose. One method is by investing into people they want to help: family members, friends, or acquaintances. Another way of using excess capital to help others, which is becoming increasingly popular, is *purposeful investing*.

MicroVest is one example of a company that invests with economic and societal purpose. MicroVest is an asset manager with $300 million in assets and has direct investments in thirty-nine countries. It invests into financial companies in developing countries with the goal of increasing the capital available to entrepreneurs. MicroVest's mission is not to maximize risk-adjusted returns; it is to provide social benefits and earn strong returns while doing so.

Mark Zuckerberg, CEO and cofounder of Facebook, also plans to invest with purpose. He made news recently when he announced he is giving 99 percent of his money to a Limited Liability Company he will run with his wife. Unlike a nonprofit, the LLC will be able to invest for-profit, make political donations, and spend money on lobbying. In other words, he will be able to pursue purposeful investing. More philanthropists and investors should consider following this path since it allows greater flexibility in how the funds can be used.

There are also growing numbers of angel investors and venture capital funds that look to invest in areas with specific societal benefits. These investors want profits, but they are willing to give up some profits, or take on more risks, in order to help society. These efforts fortunately get a lot of support from business leaders, politicians, and the local media.

You might not think of Starbucks as "purposeful" in the charitable sense, but how many jobs do you think Starbucks has created? As of 2016 it employs nearly 160,000 people and created thousands more jobs for companies that are suppliers to Starbucks. In his book, *Pour Your Heart Into It*, CEO Howard Schultz describes his experience raising start-up capital for the coffee shop chain. He said in the course of a year he spoke to 242 people and 217 told him *no*. The prospective investors would listen to his hour-long presentation, then not call him back and ignore his phone calls. Schultz said it was a very humbling time getting rejection after rejection.[1]

Howard Schultz didn't go through this humbling experience to create jobs, he did it to create a successful business and make profits (*Forbes* magazine estimates his net worth at $3 billion). The investors into Starbucks also didn't risk their capital to help create jobs, they invested to make profits. Employees and customers are the great benefactors of this search for profits by Howard Schultz and his investors. There are few, if any, better ways to help low-skilled workers than creating jobs for them with competitive pay and benefits.

Government programs and nonprofits are created to solve the problems of today, but businesses and entrepreneurs also play a pivotal role. A charity, for example, will focus on giving food to families, while Walmart, Kmart, and Aldi's work on lowering the cost of food items to remain competitive, which makes food more affordable to low-income families. Taxpayers provide welfare for the poor, but it is the business that employs the poor person and provides him or her with an income.

Purposeful investing is not meant to marginalize the indispensable nonprofit and government programs, such as foster care and special needs care. There is also no doubt that nonprofits fill a societal needs-gap where businesses don't enter and the government doesn't belong. For example, Doctors Without Borders is an organization that serves an important purpose by providing medical attention for those in the most destitute areas of the world. Obviously this would not be a successful for-profit business, therefore Doctors Without Borders relies on donations.

The benefits of entrepreneurship, nonprofits, and government programs are widely known. Purposeful investing doesn't get the attention it deserves, and I hope this brief introduction inspires greater interest.

Note

1. Howard Schultz, *Pour Your Heart Into It* (New York: Hyperion, 1997), 73.

Frequently Asked Questions

What are the most important things to remember about forever investing?

1. Purchase businesses with a target holding period of forever.
2. Favor high-quality businesses with durable competitive advantages.
3. Favor companies with outstanding management and a track record for prudent reinvestment of cash flow.
4. When you see a once-in-a-decade opportunity, buy a lot of it.
5. Don't be inflexible. Circumstances change over time and eventually there may be a good reason to exit a business.
6. Only buy when the price is attractive.

Is everyone capable of being a forever investor?

No, there are a few reasons not to be a forever investor:

1. You don't understand accounting and financial statement analysis.
2. You don't have the time to research businesses.
3. You react emotionally from sharp drops or rises in stock prices.

Should every capable investor be a forever investor?

Not necessarily, people have different talents. If you're Donald Trump you should probably stick to investing in real estate. If you're Bill Gross or Jeffery Gundlach, you should probably stick to investing in fixed income.

Can I lose money as a forever investor?

Of course. There is no investment strategy in equities that is guaranteed not to lose you money when the execution is poor. Owning stock indexes for twenty years or longer is the only equity-investment strategy that is close to risk-free.

Forever is a long time. It is an eternity. It sounds inflexible.

The *target* holding period is forever, but that doesn't mean you will own every business for the rest of your life. If circumstances for the business change, your investment thesis must change. Intelligent forever investors are adaptable.

As a forever investor, if I have an IRA, and a stock that I buy goes up 30 percent within a month of the purchase, should I sell it and buy it back later at a better price?

No. Some of the biggest investment mistakes are when investors sell great businesses after quick gains.

There is no guarantee the company will sell at a better price in the future; it may stay at the current level or continue to go up. No one can determine short-term price movements.

Short-term price predictions are never a reason to buy or sell a forever investment. It doesn't matter if the stock declines 30 percent and goes back to your original purchase price; what matters is the long-term returns.

How do I find a money manager who is a forever investor?

There are very few forever investors who are money managers, and many are not talented at it because they diversify so widely that their returns aren't much different from that of the stock market. Investors can be talented or untalented at executing their strategy, so you shouldn't blindly select any money manager.

I am a money manager who uses separately managed accounts (SMAs) to manage client funds. Compared to mutual funds and hedge funds, SMAs offer more transparency, lower fees, and greater liquidity. For more information check out www.foreverinvesting.com.

Are you afraid forever investing will become too popular?

No, if you own a concentrated portfolio of businesses forever, what others are doing doesn't matter much.

Is it better to control a company or have a non-controlling interest?

It all depends. If there is outstanding management, the benefits of a non-controlling interest are higher because of the greater liquidity if you want to purchase more shares or reduce your stake. If the management needs to be improved or you think free cash flow can be better employed, it is advantageous to have a controlling interest.

How many companies should a forever investor own?

The weight you give to each investment matters more than the number of investments you have. A portfolio of one hundred stocks can be more concentrated than a portfolio of twenty-five stocks. If you have one hundred investments and your top six ideas make up 80 percent of your assets, you are more concentrated than an investor who equally weights twenty-five stocks.

There is no magic formula for asset allocation; however, all the best forever investors have invested heavily when a rare opportunity comes along.

Should I invest into large-cap companies?

If you invest into one of the largest companies in the United States, your opportunity for great gain is not high over long periods unless you purchase it during an unusual time, such as the bottom of the market in 2009.

Midcap companies are often more attractive forever investments because they can have strong competitive advantages, solid organic growth, and opportunities to make acquisitions that can fuel growth. Companies under a $1 billion market cap tend to have weaker competitive advantages unless they operate in niche products or services; however, small caps have the greatest long-term opportunity to add value through future acquisitions. There should be extra emphasis put on the quality of management when investing into a small-cap company.

Should I take "starter positions"?

Starter positions are small initial positions in a company that investors take when they feel there is too much uncertainty for a large position at the present moment. The uncertainty can be because the investor wants to learn more about the company, there is a large event in the near future that will have a big impact on the stock price, or the investor thinks there might be downside to the stock price and he or she wants to buy more on the way down. Very large investors also take starter positions to avoid pushing up the price of the stock during the buying process.

There is nothing wrong with starter positions. Many of my starter positions, however, have had large increases shortly after I purchased them and I was no longer interested in buying more at a 30 percent higher price. The worst thing that can happen to a starter position is that it immediately goes up. Brilliant timing only has an impact if you allocate a meaningful percentage of your capital to the investment.

I have twenty years until I retire and then I need that money to be invested into income-generating assets to fund my retirement income. Should I invest into a stock index or forever investments?

The risk of the stock market having negative returns over a twenty-year period is extremely small; however, that doesn't guarantee that your returns will be above that of corporate bonds or another asset class.

Another consideration is that after fifteen years you will only have five years until retirement. Should you still be entirely invested into stocks for only five years? Probably not because anything can happen in five years.

If you only have a twenty-year horizon, you should gradually shift money from stocks to another asset class, such as real estate or bonds, every year until you are completely out of stocks within a few years of retirement.

For more information check out www.thriftyinvesting.com. Thrifty Investing focuses on suitability, diversification, low fees, and managing volatility.

Most of the top investors in the United States today are white, male, and Jewish or Christian. Where are the Women, Blacks, Hispanics, Asians, and Muslims?

This is a question people often refrain from answering with candor out of fear from backlash if something is interpreted as offensive. Often when someone tries to answer a question like this it gets them into serious trouble, because words are twisted and deemed insensitive. In other words, smart people trying to help are silenced from being more open and frank out of fear of a backlash.

As an example, Sheryl Sandberg, the Chief Operating Officer at Facebook, wrote a book called *Lean In* about women and moving up the corporate ladder. There were many vocal critics of the book, and I am not sure a male's reputation would have remained intact if he wrote that same book.

Investment results are entirely based on merit. Investing is the most level-playing field anyone could ask for. A stock does not go up or down because you are White, Black, Asian, Hispanic, Male, Female, Jewish, Muslim, or Christian. If you are a talented investor, the results will speak for themselves.

If I had to give a simple answer to why there aren't as many top women investors, my guess is that it is because more men attempt to become *great* investors than women. I've read studies that show, on average, women are better investors than men. The studies claim more men are overconfident and the really poor performers among men bring the average for the men down. In other words, the best investors are men and the worst investors are men, but women as a group perform better than men.

While investment results are entirely based on merit, money managers may face discrimination or bias when trying to attract clients. However, there are also a lot of family offices, institutions, foundations, and high-net-worth people who are biased *toward* women and minorities and want to help them succeed.

Indian-born Nehal Chopra is a bright and successful woman hedge-fund manager in her thirties. Her fund reached a peak of $1 billion in investments in 2015. One of her fund's investors is the New York state retirement system, which invested money earmarked for women and minority-run investment firms.

Fred Cummings is an African American long/short hedge-fund manager in Cleveland who focuses entirely on investing into bank stocks. He spent twenty years as a bank analyst and sticks to companies in the center of his circle of competence. Fred started his firm, Elizabeth Park Capital Management, in 2008 with only $3 million in assets. After phenomenal performance in 2008 and 2009, the fund grew rapidly. In 2015 his fund managed over $300 million. Despite receiving very little money earmarked for minority investors, Fred has been able to attract plenty of new investors.

While there is no shortage of money managers in the United States, it would be great to see more women and minority money managers.